Sudden Impact on the Job

Susan Quandt

Sudden Impact on the Job

Top Business Leaders Reveal the Secrets to Fast Success

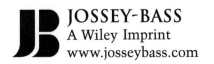

JOSSEY-BASS
A Wiley Imprint
www.josseybass.com

Published by Jossey-Bass
A Wiley Imprint
989 Market Street, San Francisco, CA 94103-1741   www.josseybass.com

Jossey-Bass books and products are available through most bookstores. To contact Jossey-Bass directly call our Customer Care Department within the U.S. at 800-956-7739, outside the U.S. at 317-572-3986, or fax 317-572-4002.

Jossey-Bass also publishes its books in a variety of electronic formats. Some content that appears in print may not be available in electronic books.

Library of Congress Cataloging-in-Publication Data

Quandt, Susan, 1954-
  Sudden impact on the job : top business leaders reveal the secrets to fast success / by Susan Quandt.
      p. cm.
Includes bibliographical references and index.
  ISBN-13: 978-0-7879-7838-9 (cloth)
  ISBN-10: 0-7879-7838-8 (cloth)
  1. Executives. 2. Chief executive officers. 3. Success in business. I. Title.
  HD38.2.Q36 2007
  658.4'09—dc22   2006017861

Printed in the United States of America
FIRST EDITION
HB Printing   10 9 8 7 6 5 4 3 2 1

Contents

To Steve,
my bashert and unwavering partner in all life's endeavors

To Ray,
the father who always thought his daughter could do
whatever she set her mind to

To Ruth,
my mother and lifelong mentor, who passed during the writing of this book.
She instilled in me wisdom, courage, and strength
as I encountered life and leadership challenges by suggesting

"What's the worst thing that can happen to you?"
or
"Always put the best construction on everything."

INTRODUCTION

So You're the New Kid on the Block

What if you walked into the offices of your new executive job—dressed to impress and ready to take the helm—only to discover that the incumbent was still in place? How would you like to enter your first board meeting and find that your directors won't introduce themselves to you or even shake your hand? Or what if within two weeks on the job you realized you had to fire most of your executive team—and you did? And what if you decided to make your first strategic investment in a promising joint venture, only to learn that one of the most notorious white-collar defendants of the year would be a stockholder in the deal?

You might think that anyone who's made it to a high-level executive job would know, instinctively or through hard-won experience, what to do in any of these scenarios—and even to have anticipated them in the first place. But in my interviews over the last several years with the country's top CEOs, I have learned that this is not the case. In fact, most of these executives walked onto the job with a lot of misconceptions about what a high-level position would be like. Why? To paraphrase Jim McNerney, now CEO of aircraft manufacturer Boeing: Although most people assume that any executive in a new position already knows how to play the game, the reality is that it usually feels like starting all over again. After all, it's a brand-new playing field with all new rules.

In these pages you will learn about the real-life experiences of corporate executives in their first 18 months on the new job. Through candid interviews with prominent new CEOs, you will learn about the problems that some of the world's highest-profile

1

business leaders bumped up against—and what they did about them. The book gives firsthand insights on where to anticipate some of the biggest surprises that blindsided even these seasoned executives and how to avoid some of the greatest mistakes they made. It will provide the context of the challenges these leaders faced and how each managed through them—often by contradicting the traditional must-do advice for executive success. While debunking certain long-held beliefs about how to succeed, the book will illuminate the most strategic information executives need to perform well—on the job or even before they start the job.

For example, some executives devise extensive game plans before walking into their new job—only to discover that the world is changing too quickly to implement the plan. Other CEOs confess that in their top positions in the corporate hierarchy, life is more public than they expected, and they need to be careful about whom they ask for advice. The old adage is true: It's lonely at the top. Given the competitiveness of corporate politics and the public nature of their jobs, CEOs sometimes find it difficult to confide in peers or board members about particularly pesky problems, especially when they are new on the job. Former mentors, especially for executives recruited from other companies, are not immersed in the new circumstances and thus are unable to offer helpful insights.

Yet at the same time that executives are dealing with so many challenges in their new jobs, the stakes they face are higher than they've ever been before. The United States has only recently begun to emerge from a decade of high unemployment—and executive ranks were among the hardest hit. In the first half of 2005 alone, more than 770 CEOs left their jobs—a full 90% higher than turnover the previous year.[1] And according to one survey, with the easing of the job market, a whopping 96% of currently employed senior executives expect to change companies within a year.[2] Another survey of middle managers found that 48% were currently job hunting or planned to start looking as the job market improves.[3]

It seems that the average executive, therefore, is having to stare down much uncertainty, and probably frustration, in finding the right job. Those executives lucky enough to find a job are desperate to succeed and make an impact on their new organization as swiftly and effectively as possible. Taken all together, these current realities lead to even more stress on newly hired executives to do the right thing—right away.

This book will help you make that kind of immediate impact. In it you will find the best advice I have extracted from my interviews with the country's most successful CEOs, sharing the myths they believed when they entered their jobs—and the realities they encountered during their first days and months. The leaders I talked to work in a range of industry sectors including high-tech, financial, manufacturing, consumer goods, chemicals, publishing, retail, and telecommunications. I asked them everything from how they snared their present jobs to what their early formidable challenges were. These business pros shared what they thought the priorities were before starting their new positions and what they learned once they entered the executive suite. They talked to me candidly about what worked and what didn't. They revealed the flawed assumptions they made during the hiring process and the early surprises they confronted.[4]

For example, Ed Zander recounts the story of joining Motorola—and how he was able to make his impact there. Dave Dorman, recently retired chairman and CEO of AT&T, relates how in choosing members for your team you never want a left-handed shortstop. Stephanie Streeter of Banta recounts her experience as a "West Coast girl" becoming CEO of a major Midwestern company located in a town of fewer than 20,000. Jamie Dimon (now CEO of JP Morgan Chase) describes how to overcome loneliness at the top and ultimately wildly succeed, after entering a less than welcoming environment at Bank One. Pat Russo of Lucent shares how she recovered when the best-laid of plans crumbled as the market bottom dropped beyond any expectation.

While other books attempt to provide a theoretical template, or "key factors for success" that assume that every job and every company will fit their 90- or 100-day plan, my approach is different:

I believe that the challenge for you, as it was for the CEOs I interviewed, is that what worked on your last job won't always work in your new position. Templates and road maps that rely on historical data may not prove helpful now. Accordingly, this book is not a list of organizational theories postulated by a management guru; rather, you'll find here the real-life experiences of leaders who have succeeded along their career paths to arrive at the rarest of jobs, CEO—and then succeeded at that.

Even so, this book is not solely for new or aspiring CEOs. Instead, it offers a hands-on guide to proven solutions—for any high-level executive and in situations that occur across companies and industries. As a result, this book also provides unusual insights into how to manage your career toward the top job in your company or upward in your industry, your department, or your field.

In my interviews with CEOs, common themes emerged again and again around what I've come to see as seven misconceptions, or myths, about how to succeed in a top executive position. We've all heard them at one time or another. These are the things we read about in the business press—or hear the gurus say—things that top executives get told they should do for sudden impact on a new job. I have framed the book around these myths, which are as follows:

Myth #1: High-impact executives encounter no surprises when stepping into their new position.

Myth #2: High-impact executives walk into the job with a solid game plan.

Myth #3: High-impact executives play it safe and get to know their new teams before making changes.

Myth #4: High-impact executives never make mistakes.

Myth #5: High-impact executives are lone rangers who no longer need mentoring and advice.

Myth #6: High-impact executives always quicken the pace of the organization for best results.

Myth #7: High-impact executives need to make a major mark on their companies by the end of their first 90 days.

Each chapter focuses on one of these myths and explores the experiences and insights about the realities the CEOs I interviewed actually confronted. Chapter One looks at a common myth in business: that great executives come into their new positions knowing exactly what to expect. The CEOs I spoke with were candid about the many surprises they encountered in their new jobs—and the surprising ways their new companies fell short in helping them get acclimated.

Chapter Two focuses on the second myth, supported by much of the business literature: Do all high-level executives come into the job with a game plan, ready to execute? A candid discussion ensues on how the CEOs I spoke with introduced change and, with 20-20 hindsight, what they would do differently. They share what methods worked for them in early identification of priorities as well as how they spotted potential traps.

Chapter Three takes on the third myth, that the best new executives get to know their new team before making changes. All savvy new executives know that to be successful, the culture of the organization has to be supportive of their initiatives. While organizational experts often caution that executives should take their time before making changes in the incumbent team, circumstances can dictate making change quickly, sometimes from within and other times from the outside and—sometimes it even involves taking over all the reins yourself for a while. The CEOs I interviewed share their insider impressions on how and when to continue the existing culture or environment and what are the triggers for change.

Chapter Four addresses the widely held belief that the best executives never make mistakes. Several of the CEOs I spoke with confessed to having regrets. Still, given the leadership literature that tells us effective leaders are typically optimists, it's not surprising that they saw mistakes as opportunities for learning and improvising on the job. Being excellent problem solvers by nature, the same executives also shared their ways of compensating for their regrets as well as alternate paths to success. Best of all, the CEOs here share what they themselves would do over if they could.

Chapter Five takes a look at the belief that successful executives are at the top of their game and don't need others' insights, camaraderie, or mentoring. The CEOs I interviewed said they relied on creative approaches to problem solving and shared secrets to their success that don't appear in most résumés. Their examples cite how they find wisdom and support from peers, friends, and professional associations—and in some unconventional places.

Chapter Six addresses the question: Is faster always better? Should high-level executives necessarily quicken the pace of their new organizations? Again, depending on the context of their succession to the new job, new leaders provided some surprising answers to that debate. They also related what they feel is the rhythm of their organizations—and how their own rhythms affect results.

Chapter Seven examines what is probably the most common belief about top executives new to their positions: that they must make a major mark on their company by the end of their first 90 days. Although some CEOs trigger major change right away, often their biggest impact comes later in the game. Some leaders did indeed believe that early wins were essential and should be strategically choreographed, and the chapter looks at the places where new executives turned for those early wins—employees? customers? investors? All of the above? Meanwhile, other CEOs I spoke with did not think that such early wins were the most crucial component of success on the new job, and they offer their insights as to why. Thus perhaps the biggest myth of all is the title of the book— *Sudden Impact* as an overarching measure of success. Instead, certain accomplishments can be early or sudden while others, to be effective or meaningful, will take time, fortitude, and understanding the rhythm of the organization you lead.

In Chapter Eight, the book's conclusion, the realities that emerged from the CEOs' stories will be juxtaposed against the myths from the chapters—and you will find tips on how to carve out your own best path in the first days and months on the new job.

Finally, ten of the CEOs I interviewed offer you the three key pieces of advice they wanted any new executive to have as they climb the career ladder of success.

Taken together, these chapters offer what any aspiring CEO or new kid on the executive block would wish for—and would be unlikely to find in the real world: the experience of sitting down and chatting with people who have walked the path you're on now—an opportunity to hear their personal stories. The CEOs in this book tell you about the twists and turns you'll encounter on the new job, as well as the life-saving techniques that worked for them in the face of what at times seemed like insurmountable challenges. They offer firsthand insights about where to anticipate some of the biggest surprises that blindsided even these seasoned executives, and how to avoid some of the greatest mistakes they made.

Ultimately, the advice these CEOs offer will help you develop your own game plan, formally or informally, for becoming the most effective and highest-impact executive you possibly can be. Let's begin with a look at Myth #1, and whether or not the best, the most resourceful, and most clearly destined-for-success executives always walk into the job knowing exactly what to expect.

1

GOT IT!

Myth #1: High-impact executives encounter no
surprises when stepping into their new position.

When Bank One came calling, it was an offer Jamie Dimon couldn't refuse.[1] First of all, he hadn't worked for a while. He had plenty of job offers, but he was waiting for the right one. As he was talking to Bank One, he realized that in spite of some drawbacks—like having to move his family from New York to Chicago—he wanted to join the company. He knew financial services well. And really, how many large banks come calling to offer you a job as CEO? He was 44 years old, and he thought, if you're given an opportunity like that, you don't get to pick and choose all the details—like the fact that, at the time, Bank One was in trouble. With a recession looming, Dimon knew he'd have to move quickly to turn it around. He truly needed to have a sudden impact.

So when Dimon arrived for his first day on the job, he was hoping for a positive beginning—and then to hit the ground running. Instead, he felt blocked at every turn. Dimon is often characterized by the press as a gunslinger, but my first impression of him when we met at Bank One's executive offices for our interview was that of a regular guy—a banker not even wearing a suit—with an open demeanor and relatively easy-going manner. The "dynamo" the press often cites could be seen in his intense, active listening. You can almost feel his mind accessing data in nanoseconds as he listens to you. A charismatic man of unpredictable yet decisive action, he was exactly what Bank One needed—even if some members of the board weren't ready to fully support his tenure in the beginning.

Indeed, his tough first day on the job began with a board meeting. With a total board membership of 19 at the time, only six board members stood to shake his hand. The rest didn't greet him at all. He sat down and said, "My name is Jamie." That was the extent of his welcome and introduction.

He'd read in the newspaper that many of the older board members were against him and had lobbied for Bank One's interim CEO to take the position permanently. But since he also knew that ultimately he was the unanimous choice, he simply hadn't expected such a frosty welcome. What's more, no one offered to show him to his office. At the end of the meeting, as the board members were getting up to leave, Dimon himself had to ask: "So where's my office?" Someone pointed him in the vague direction of a big corner office that had belonged to the acting CEO. Dimon didn't want to take it but said, "OK." He even had to track down the HR guy himself to get an executive assistant. A bad first day indeed for a guy who had made his daughters change cities and schools for this job, as well as having left his parents—and weekly family dinners that had been important to them all—behind in New York.

The CEOs I interviewed for this book didn't all encounter such chilling surprises as the in-your-face rejection Dimon received on his first day at work. But the reality is that even high-level executives like CEOs don't often walk into the job holding all the cards. Surprises can and do await them—and how they deal with the unexpected can mean the difference between making a sudden impact or not. Several factors come into play, but one of the biggest is how their succession occurred.

Succession Matters

The circumstances of becoming CEO are as varied as the people in the job. Some came up through a series of promotions within the organization; what Ed Zander of Motorola would call "growing organically." Others parachute into the top job, usually in times of leadership crisis manifested by unexpected negative financial indicators—flat earnings, falling revenues, or stagnant growth. And while most new CEOs enter the job with the board's unanimous approval, some come in with reluctant board support, which clearly affects their first days on the job, as Jamie Dimon learned all too well.

Those who have risen organically—meaning they were already working in the company when they were offered the top job—often have the benefit of a break-in period so they usually face relatively few surprises (although we'll see at least one exception to this rule in this chapter—the case of the sudden death of one CEO). Usually, they were first promoted to chief operating officer or president with the implicit, or sometimes explicit, understanding that CEO would be the next step. When explicit, the designated leader has an incredible advantage in proactively selecting his or her future team and both influencing and planning change to the organization and its strategy. In contrast, most CEOs parachuting in from outside the company have little luxury of time, planning, or contemplation and can find themselves caught completely off-guard.

Parachuting In

The following stories highlight how three CEOs got their jobs from the outside—and the kinds of surprises that can go hand-in-hand with such situations. They also show where additional information might have helped these CEOs, and cases where no matter how much information a candidate has before accepting a position, sometimes nothing can replace being there to understand the true realities of the job.

Ed Zander, CEO, Motorola.   Believe it or not, given his current high-profile enthusiasm in the press, this is the story of a reluctant CEO. In fact, when Ed Zander took the helm at Motorola at age 56, the move was such a turn in the road from where Zander thought his career—and the rest of his life—was going that he still has very strong recall of the whole series of events.

Like most business executives, Zander noticed in the *Wall Street Journal* in October 2003 that the CEO of Motorola had left over concerns about the company's financial performance. Little did

Zander realize at the time the personal implications for him of that announcement. He took special note only because he knew Motorola. In a previous role as chief operating officer at Sun Microsystems, Zander had gotten to know people at Motorola because Sun was a big supplier to them.

Soon a prominent headhunter called Zander and inquired about his interest in the job. At the time, he was managing director at Silver Lake Partners, a private equity fund specializing in technology investments. Zander, an outspoken, friendly, fast-talking New York native who looooves to tell a story, says that he was enjoying his role as investor and adviser to other companies. Then another big headhunter called who was competing to fill the job. Zander laughs, "They call guys like me and say, would you consider whatever hot job is available and then they walk into the hiring company and say, 'I can get Ed for this job.' That's what goes on. When the headhunters called about Motorola, I quickly said no, no, no! Then I made a mistake. I had dinner with some of Motorola's board members because they were pretty incredible guys who I thought it would be cool to meet."

The dinner, arranged by Jim Citrin, an executive recruiter from Spencer Stuart, would include John Pepper, who was the lead director on the search committee and former Procter & Gamble CEO, and Larry Fuller, the former Amoco (now part of British Petroleum) CEO. Zander lived on the West Coast in Silicon Valley but he had a home in Boston near his wife's family. He happened to be in Boston at the time, and Pepper and Fuller were willing to fly there just to have dinner with him. How could anyone turn down a simple dinner? Zander says Citrin shrewdly appealed to Zander's weakness—his tendency to be a sucker for getting in on something interesting—and he thought these two men were particularly interesting leaders. Whether Zander wanted the job or not, he thought it was worth dinner to meet the former P&G and Amoco CEOs.

Sunday night arrived and Zander was meeting them at 7 P.M. He remembers leaving his place, and just like any job candidate, worrying about dropping food on his suit. He even had a Motorola phone with him, which he'd actually bought long before there was any idea of meeting with Motorola.

As Zander recalls the dinner, "The interesting thing is I had no intention of taking the job so I was talking like I'm talking to anybody—I wasn't there interviewing. It wasn't like I was pressured. I told them what I thought about Motorola, about my life, and that I wasn't interested in the job—couldn't move my family to Chicago. They kept asking me questions about Motorola. John asked, 'What do you think Motorola could stand for in the next couple of years? What should we do?' I said, 'Look, I don't even know the company. I can't tell you that.' Then I looked down and I saw the little "M" on my phone and ad-libbed, 'You know, you've got it right in front of you. See that little "M"?' They said yeah. I said, 'It stands for Mobility. It stands for mobility—not wireless—there's a difference. You've got to *own* mobile communications—that's where the future is going.' Later on they told me they thought that was really something."

When Jim Citrin called him after the dinner to ask him to consider the job, Zander told him to leave him alone. "Then I started thinking about it. That's the trouble—you start thinking." Zander thought about his life. He was still relatively young. He liked private equity but did miss the hands-on operational part at Sun. Zander's thought process about accepting the job was very similar to that of other CEOs that I interviewed for this book. He reflected on the fact that you are dealt a hand in your life. He was being considered for leadership of a Fortune 50 company. How many people get that opportunity? There are 50 people running Fortune 50 companies and over 20 years, he speculated, there are only a few hundred—at most—people who get the opportunity.

Zander said, "Somebody said to me, 'You've never been a CEO. It's a leap of faith on their part to do this.' I wasn't going to get the chance at Sun, and there was no other big job on the West Coast that I liked."

This was similar to what other new CEOs told me they recalled about being offered the top job. At some point the idea comes alive for them. The possibilities occupy their waking thoughts during the process. Candidates get "juiced" about how they can make a difference in such a position and what a truly unique opportunity is being held out to them. Zander soon found himself accepting another interview and then another. He couldn't talk to a lot of people because of the secrecy of Motorola's search. He sought the advice of a couple of very close friends. He would go through "what if" scenarios of taking or not taking the job. Zander says the early advice broke into two camps. There were some who said you can't pass this up even if you can't turn it around, because, as Zander himself had concluded, how many people were going to get to do this? These friends said just do it—go for it. You don't need the approval. You don't need the money. You don't need the "things." Do it because it's just a great thing to go do—and Chicago's not that bad.

The other camp told Zander he was crazy. They said that the Motorola culture was too ingrained. It was too far gone for him to turn it around. Zander said they gave him twenty reasons not to do it.

In spite of the twenty reasons, Zander proceeded with more interviews—very quickly—in November. He never got to visit with any employees at Motorola headquarters. Besides Pat Canavan, who was the inside executive at Motorola involved with the CEO search, Zander got to talk with only two other executives: on the phone twice with one of the division heads, Greg Brown, and in person once with the chief technical officer, Padmasree Warrior. Most of his interviewing occurred with board members.

The board was tough. Even though Zander was relatively well known in the corporate world, the interviews were not a mere formality. There was a lot of pressure on Motorola's board to make sure that they were getting the right candidate, especially since he'd be coming from outside. Zander's predecessor had been part of the company's founding family and the company's COO at the time had been recruited from General Electric's repertory of high potential leaders with an expectation of future growth at Motorola. The board wanted to assure themselves, their shareholders, and the Motorola team that they had truly put in the effort to achieve their goal, so they really grilled him. Zander remembers a particularly tough session in New York. They asked him questions like "What went wrong at Sun?" He described it as a "free-flowing six-on-one thing" for nearly three hours. He left feeling drained and not optimistic.

It was the Thanksgiving holiday and Zander was on his way to his son's house in New Jersey. When he got there he told his family that he was not going to get the job after that interview. John Pepper called Zander at five o'clock the same day, which Zander thought signaled a brush-off. Instead, Pepper told him the board had a caucus about the other candidates and they wanted to offer him the job. Zander was astounded. Immediately upon hanging up, Zander went downstairs to tell his family. His wife, his two sons, his sister, and his mother (who has since passed away) were there. Zander's mother was 95 at the time and blind.

Zander assembled everyone in the living room. He said, "I got an offer. If I take this job, it's going to change our lives. I won't have as much time as I do now or have the chance to be with my sons again. I'm going to be stressed. It'll be hard: lots of traveling and I may not be successful. My name is going to be in the press. They're going to pick at me, I'm going to get nailed, I'm going to be appraised, I'm going to get abused in this day and age." He laid out all the pros and cons and said they were all going to vote on it.

Zander gave his family a chance to think about it. He remembered going out by the pool at his son's home and his mother was out there alone. His mother had been telling him for twenty years to slow down, to stop working so hard. He asked her what he should do. He will never forget her response. She said, "Go do it, Eddie. You've got to do it. You should try it. I think you have to. I know it's crazy that I would say this." Zander was shocked, surprised, and very moved that she told him just the opposite of what he expected.

When they reconvened to vote, one of Zander's sons voted against it. He said not to do it because of the concerns Zander had raised about the time demands and quality-of-life issues. Zander thinks his son was afraid because, even though he was grown by then, he remembered growing up watching his father being immersed at Sun and how hard that had been for him. Yet, given the support of all the other family members, Zander decided to move forward.

Zander called Pepper back that night. Motorola's formal offer and subsequent negotiations took several weeks. Zander chose to stay out of that process. Ever the hard-charging executive, he was already busy getting ready for the job. He got all the Motorola data he could get from the company and also sought out every analyst report available. He says "immersion" best describes his initiation for the job into which he was about to parachute under tough circumstances. He believes he gathered information from every source he could. He gathered nearly every piece of information written about Motorola. He talked to people who were CEOs elsewhere and read books by others. He talked to people who had experience with Motorola, on the inside and on the outside. He sought out Pat Russo at Lucent and Mike Cappellas at MCI, both of whom dropped in at the top. Some of the other influential people he talked to were John Chambers at Cisco and Steve Jobs at Apple, who's a personal friend. He talked to a "whole bunch of people" about management and leadership, what they did when they were new, and what mistakes they made. He read books, including those by former CEOs Larry Bossidy, Lou Gerstner, and Jack Welch. Zander exhausted every avenue to data on Motorola and the challenges of a new CEO. Zander said he analyzed his new job like we've all been told we should do—what should happen during the first 90 days and the first six months. He had a first 100 days plan: *not* to plan, but rather to learn, listen, and not undertake any major initiative.

Then, once his appointment was announced on December 16, 2003, he talked to his executive team about the new Motorola. Zander met with them that evening at the company's headquarters in Schaumburg, Illinois, a suburb about 45 minutes northwest of downtown Chicago. He thinks he came in a little more prepared than what they had expected. He spoke to them about who he was: "'This is what I like. This is what I don't. This is my style. This is the good and the bad about Ed Zander. You can Google me if you want.' Then I said, 'Here is your homework assignment over Christmas—to tell me about your business.' It wasn't very hard. It was very simple. I didn't say anything about the business. I didn't get into what the issues were. I finished by telling them what I wanted to do in January."

During this period, in his continuing quest for information, Zander met with some people who were former executives at the company. He'd ask them to start out by giving him the good, the bad, and the ugly, and they did—and he took copious notes. To Zander, having as much information as possible is crucial. He believes that one of the reasons he got the job after that last three-hour grueling interview in New York was that he had unbelievable data on the company. "Not just numbers and stuff, but insights into the businesses. They just couldn't believe how prepared I was. They told me later that was the difference between me and the other candidates. I had really done my work on knowing the challenges and opportunities, plus potential issues for each of the divisions and businesses, plus a little bit about the culture. I had compiled my thoughts from those early talks with friends when I asked them what they thought I should do if Motorola offered me the job."

After the announcement in December, he was able to talk more freely with people. He remembered that people seemed to come out of the woodwork—all of his friends weighed in. Like him, Zander says, his friends say what's on their minds. And again, as it had earlier in the process, the advice he got came down in two camps. Some said, "Ed, you're screwed." Others said, "Ed, you'll be great." Many warned that he was really sticking his neck out—and they hoped it wouldn't be cut off.

Finally, Zander took two weeks off over Christmas to be with his family one last time before he started the new job. "I came back in January. I laid low the first 100 days. Then I told my team more about the first six months."

Of all the CEOs I interviewed, Zander probably had done the most primary and secondary research on his new company and the CEO job. If anyone seemed to have covered all the bases and then some, it was Ed Zander. Yet, even with such a high level of preparation and planning, Zander found himself caught off-guard about the actual job vs. his expectations from the interview process.

"The biggest surprise, the one that really floored me when I started work that January, was the lack of customer focus," said Zander. Executive involvement in delighting customers, improving customer satisfaction, and developing closer relationships was nonexistent. To begin to resolve the need for more customer focus, Zander began visiting customers himself—something past CEOs had rarely done.

"I was here two or three weeks and no one had asked me to call a customer, which I thought was weird," he recalls. "It was almost three or four weeks into the job so I called someone and said who are our top customers? What do we sell to them? They gave me the list. I think number one was Nextel. I started dialing the phone right there.

"The customer relationships were—to some extent, some of them still are—just unbelievably bad. I walked into some customers and the first thing they'd say is 'Hi, Ed,' in a very nice way. They'd welcome me and then beat the living crap out of me. I came home in January and February and I was mortified. I kept saying to myself, 'holy mackerel!' Relationships were just so beaten up, with lots of mistrust."

Another way Zander encouraged his organization to get more focused on customers was to change the compensation program midyear. As he recalls, "Even though the compensation program was designed in February of last year, I made a change and put 10–15% of the bonus around quality and customer satisfaction—which was a big fight because they never measured that. I heard complaints, 'What are you doing to my bonus?' I wanted to make it 100%. That's how aggravated I was. The first thing needs to be recognition of who's paying for the lights around here. We don't sell unless people buy and they don't buy unless we make them happy. Very simple things." Another simple thing Zander instituted was assigning an executive sponsor to each customer.

Still, today, Zander admits he does not get many calls from his sales force to go on customer visits. He finds it strange but thinks the culture is changing and they are getting better at it. Until they do, Zander just keeps doing it himself.

The second big surprise for Zander was that his new team wasn't a team in the way he was used to working with one. He is a West Coast guy used to telling it like it is and having others do the same back at him. He knew management styles were different in different places and tried not to pass judgment on Motorola's previous leadership. "The way I grew up in business, you sit in a room with ten, twelve people. You basically decide, not only what the numbers are but even the culture of the company. You decide what the compensation programs are. You decide whether you're going to buy a building. It's not consensus management. It's not participative management. You just get it done—together as a team."

Zander began to resolve the teamwork problem by midyear. He had initially promised everyone a "clean slate" for the first six months. Some team members understood Zander's agenda and excelled. Others did not. They left the company or were transferred to different positions. Unlike the commonly held belief that outsiders tend to bring in their own posse when a company is in financial crisis, Zander asserts that he primarily promoted from within but in a very few instances resorted to outsiders to fill experience and skill gaps.

When I interviewed Zander a year into the job, he laughed at the notion of sudden impact. Coming from the Silicon Valley, he thought he could come in and in three to six months have everything fixed. He recalls that the board warned and coached him on lowering his expectations. Whenever he thought he could do something in a certain time, he learned to double it or triple it. The reality is he is leading 67,000 people who have been with Motorola in many cases for 20 or 30 years and are enmeshed in doing it one way. And, not all of that way is wrong. He has to be cognizant of not throwing out the baby with the bath water. His company's culture values integrity. It values people. In turn, they try to do the right thing and there is a sense of loyalty—long term—to the company. Zander believes he has a lot of good foundational values to build on. He thinks the key to impact is starting with the good and praising what works—and then changing the things they could do better.

"The things I've focused on, time will tell. I felt that day one, I didn't even want to talk strategy for a while. To me this company just needed to do one or two things—get customer satisfaction up and customer focus up. So that's what I did. I made it a number one issue and talked about it in every meeting I was in."

At the time I interviewed Zander, Motorola had turned out five good quarters. Zander says it's execution and he can't take credit for it yet. To him it's the simple concept of saying what they're going to do and getting the numbers. "We give guidance—even internally, it's very important. It's less important to me what Wall Street thinks. Of course, I work for the shareholders, but I don't work for the financial analysts. The thing is, if you get a cadence inside your company and say this is what you're going to go do, these are the numbers you're going to go do, these are the programs you're going to share, these are the things that you adhere to—if you do that, it's like getting good manners at home. You just start to do it. You act more like a high-performance company. It was getting very measurable, definable things to do and then doing them. Then the outside takes care of itself.

"So, it's making numbers and making goals—we aren't there yet. We take two steps forward and two steps back. . . . We get some great products out and then we get a train wreck on a quality issue. We do something right, we do something wrong. It's amazing. It's going to take a while, but to me execution, customers, and quality are the things that I push really hard every day."

Zander concludes: "You start to figure out from the team—there's power right there—maybe you can go and let your hair down a little more with this person or that person. You build that kind of trust and rapport. Some of the people I thought I could trust, I misread. Some of the people went the other way—that's the single thing I miss the most by coming in from the top. You are really alone—you don't know anything about the culture. It's much harder than people will ever understand—being dropped in from the top of a big company. I wish to say—I didn't even know where the bathroom was. And I mean that in quotes because I didn't know—if you'd have asked me the first part of last year: How does somebody get promoted? How do you do titles? How do you do compensation? How do you do strategy? How do you do this? How do you price a product? Everything was like a newborn baby taking a first step and certainly joining a start-up is easier. A small company is easy, but in a company so large, so global, so architected, so decentralized, all I could do was learn."

As he foretold at the family vote, being CEO of Motorola has changed his life, and his family's. He no longer has the time he once did with his sons. The stress—and the unanticipated cultural hurdles—were even greater than expected. Zander admits the job is hard and he is traveling a lot. His name is indeed regularly in the press and there have been concerns about some product setbacks, offset by some announcements about new product development. But as far as his early fears that he might not be successful, by now most would agree that Zander doesn't have to worry about that one.

Let's look now at the story of yet another CEO who came to the job from the outside. Although Stephanie Streeter had almost two years to grow into her job as CEO of Banta Corporation, which she accepted at age forty-five, she was hired with the express commitment that she'd be groomed for the top job. Even so, she came face-to-face with a number of surprises, not the least of which began with the fact that she was dropping in from a completely different industry.

Stephanie Streeter, CEO, Banta Corporation. When Don Belcher called in August 2000, Stephanie Streeter was chief operating officer at Idealab!, a Pasadena-based high technology company that created and managed a network of companies in various stages of development. As CEO and chairman of Banta Corporation,

Belcher headed a Fortune 1000 company whose bedrock printing business serves leading publishers and direct marketers.

Belcher was calling to tell Streeter that he needed to get a successor in place because the bylaws of the corporation required him to retire at 65. Belcher was running out of time to effect a smooth leadership transition—with just 24 months and no heir apparent. It turned out that Belcher's timing was superb. Streeter's overarching business goal was to be a CEO and run her own company, and she was not having a very good experience at Idealab! She was COO but had concluded it was the wrong place for her for a number of reasons, mainly that the founder and CEO was not going to be stepping down in the foreseeable future.

Belcher and Streeter had worked together at Avery Dennison, the West Coast paper products and label manufacturer. He remembered her intellect, drive, and competitive spirit. Streeter had been captain of the women's basketball team at Stanford. She had the distinction—and disappointment—of making the U.S. Olympics women's basketball team in 1980—the year the United States boycotted the games. In spite of that, Streeter has continued her involvement with the organization and today is a member of the U.S. Olympic Committee.

When Streeter graduated from Stanford, she started her career in computer programming. Tall and thin, with the look of an athlete even when in a business suit, she has been involved in sports all her life—still coaching kids, playing volleyball, and hiking. She greets everyone with a warm smile and a twinkle in her eye, yet one can see that she is sizing up the situation at all times—just like she used to do with rival players. *Competitive* and *analytical* are two of Streeter's obvious strengths, yet she offsets them with an inclusive joie de vivre for every task she undertakes and person she meets.

At Avery Dennison Streeter's drive and competitiveness propelled her into a marketing job among other more likely recruits who had classic packaged goods marketing experience with the likes of Pillsbury and General Mills.

Streeter's claim to fame at Avery Dennison was introducing laser printer labels to the market. That may not seem like much now, but at the time, laser technology was new: there were only 500,000 laser printers out in the world at the time. It took Streeter eight months to convince her boss that the time was right. She was afraid they were going to miss the window of opportunity to be first mover in this new market. She kept telling him they had to be first. He finally relented, and the rest is history. Streeter's sense of timing was superb. Belcher hadn't forgotten either.

Initially, Belcher wanted to set up a competition between whomever he found from the outside and someone he had identified on the inside. The first job Belcher talked to Streeter about was president of the print sector, which was and is Banta's largest and most important business. Streeter wasn't interested. She let Belcher know that what she was really after was to be president or COO—something that led directly to CEO. She knew she wanted to run something and she wanted to run something big. Streeter put it all on the table during their first conversation.

It took a few months, but Belcher came back and told Streeter he had rethought everything and he wanted to offer her the position of president and COO. He said, given her great track record, he knew he was really recruiting his successor. He had eliminated the competition. He told her afterward that, in spite of the fact that she wasn't interested, he knew she was the right person and head and shoulders above anybody he had internally. He said he realized it would've been a mock competition and he wasn't going to do that to her or the other person. After more discussion, Belcher sweetened the deal to Streeter's way of thinking by giving her a timeline of 18 to 24 months to CEO. He knew he had to go at 65 so the timing was clearly delineated.

The more Streeter found out about the company, the better the fit seemed to be. She learned that besides the printing business, the corporation is also a strong player in the rapidly developing supply chain management arena, serving as a global outsourcing partner to leading companies in technology, pharmaceuticals, and medical devices. All told, the company sells nearly $1.4 billion worth of services. Headquartered in Menasha, Wisconsin, Banta employs nearly 8,000 people worldwide and boasts 40 manufacturing facilities around the world, including Mexico, Ireland, Scotland, and Singapore.

Streeter was intrigued, even though the transition from metropolitan Los Angeles and sunny California to tiny Menasha and cold Wisconsin was going to be a little traumatic, and printing wasn't a particularly interesting or sexy industry. All that aside, what most interested Streeter was a successful company, in a real business, making real money, with a number of different business models to make it challenging, if not always interesting sector to sector.

Streeter wanted to know more about the team. She made sure that she interviewed with all the people who were going to be her direct reports and she interviewed with a couple of board members. She felt she had a reasonable idea of what she was getting into. She found the company had good people, "rock solid and salt of the earth folks," which appealed to her.

Streeter arrived at Banta in January 2001, and even though she would have 21 months at Banta to prepare before taking over as CEO, she faced three surprises right off the bat. First, the company was not in as good shape as she had been led to believe. Rather than focusing on new market opportunities and revenue growth, Streeter had to dive into the thorny issues of expense cuts and headcount reductions.

Second, her style and Belcher's had diverged since working together at Avery Dennison. What she says she learned from the situation is that you can think from the interview process that you are mentally in line with somebody but, until you are in the situation "walking the talk" together, you don't realize that they go about things differently or they represent things differently from how you see them. For instance, very little external market data was being used in making decisions, and a certain complacency had crept over the organization.

The third surprise for Streeter, as for many of the other CEOs interviewed for this book, was the people legacy. The people hired by the incumbent CEO had a history with him and in his mind they were doing a great job. As Streeter says, "A longtime CEO just can't see the change that is necessary. When Don left, he had been here ten years. I hope I have the sense that if I'm not renewing the company that I'll leave after a number of years. Otherwise, you just get stale."

Aside from those three main challenges, Streeter bumped up against a few things you might expect a very competitive female CEO to run into at a traditional Midwestern company. "First, the girl thing was a big deal," she recalls, "I knew that right away—when everyone said it *wasn't* a big thing. If someone says, 'Your being a lady doesn't really bother me, I've dealt with ladies before,' you have to say to yourself, OK, your vernacular is really screwed up, so how's everything else? For the people here, I was really an anomaly. My reputation for being competitive quickly got around, and it's absolutely true. I see a set of stairs and I'll race my husband to the top. But to many people at this company, I was bizarre."

What's more, at first the people at Banta didn't seem too comfortable with the fact that Streeter asked a lot of questions. She remembers people putting their hand out and saying, "Don't ask me any more questions, because I know what I'm doing." They would imply she was new and didn't understand their business or how complicated it was. They saw their business as unique. Her solution? "I just believe in will. I wasn't going away. I'm competitive enough and willful enough that I figured I'd just outlast them. It's worked so far."

Consider now the kinds of surprises faced by one final CEO who parachuted in. In fact, you probably can't drop into a company in a more dramatic way than did John Parker, who at age 55 became CEO of American Culinary ChefsBest—by buying the company.

John Parker, CEO, American Culinary ChefsBest. It's unusual to see a CEO walking out of a pristine professional kitchen offering you a chocolate chip cookie, and John Parker says one of the best perks of the job is getting to sample the products—after the judging is completed. The mission of Parker's company, in fact, is to do such judging and to bestow its ChefsBest Award on the most deserving quality food and beverage products. Think Oscar or Emmy of the food industry.

By all accounts, John Parker is the consummate entrepreneur. Parker's salt-and-pepper hair and easy-going gait belie his days as a competitive polo player and rugged mountain climber. Parker had sold his prior successful venture, a nationwide chain of radio stations, in the mid-1990s and had taken a few well-deserved years off. But he didn't exactly laze around. He became an active member of the Explorers' Club, participating in expeditions around the world. He set out to climb the seven highest mountain summits in the world and has tackled five so far. He still plays polo, which is a very physical, active sport. He says the reason he enjoys adventure—extreme adventure, some might say—is because it brings him to the "now." Faced with a dangerous situation, he says, you totally forget everything around you and it brings you into the moment. This ability to focus his perspective clearly has contributed to Parker's current success in quickly rolling out a new business model and setting early priorities.

When Parker came across the company, he was enjoying his freedom but looking for a new challenge. After owning his own business, he had no intention of joining a publicly held corporation. So, he thought, why not buy another one? As Parker tells it in his spacious San Francisco headquarters with walls of windows overlooking ducks parading through the Levi Strauss Plaza, "The company was about twelve years old when I bought it four years ago. It was a relatively small company run by several chefs, who tasted food for restaurant chains. For instance, they would select one or two types of caviar for a restaurant chain. The chain wouldn't have the time or inclination to taste every kind of caviar, so they would hire the firm to taste all of them and find the best-tasting ones. The clients were primarily restaurant chains, airlines, and cruise lines. I came across this business and it was fascinating, one of a kind. I could see bigger potential in taking it in a different direction."

Parker took the basic concept of determining the best-tasting products and made it a very sophisticated business, changing the business model so that both the customer and what the firm taste-tests is now different but the basic concept of tasting food to determine the best products remained. Not only did Parker buy a company in an industry in which he had no experience, but on top of that, he changed the concept and he changed the brand, renaming the company American Culinary ChefsBest and introducing the award he licenses, the ChefsBest Award.

"Here was a company that had the talent for evaluating food and quantifying taste. Now it is using that quantification to evaluate competitors and determine the best-tasting product. I decided to take that concept, move it over to retail (meaning grocery products in a retail market), and develop a judging process. It's very sophisticated now and getting more so literally every six months as we take big steps forward with what we do in the taste kitchen. That's all we do. Our job is to keep getting better and better at it. I changed the business model because that was really where the company was needed—to help the consumer make the best decision." Parker's strategy seems to be succeeding. Some of his licensees include Frito-Lay, Dreyer's Ice Cream, Russell-Stover, and E&J Gallo. The ChefsBest award is now featured in TV ads for several prominent brands.

Even as Parker was putting his new company through all of these changes, Parker himself encountered a number of surprises that became his first big challenges as CEO. First was the need to educate the food industry about what American Culinary Chefs-Best did. It was a new business concept at the time; the food industry had never had an award such as the one Parker developed. He had to establish the credibility of the judging process so the industry would understand it and have the confidence in it to endorse it by putting the ChefsBest award on their packaging.

The second hurdle for Parker was just how small the organization was and how much he needed to upgrade. The company didn't even have a robust accounting system. He found receipts in a shoe box and the accounting system running on the home version of Quicken—and it was a company with several million dollars of sales. The challenge for Parker was building infrastructure, systems, technologies, people, and, most important, culture—a recurring theme among the CEOs I spoke to. He had to develop the corporate culture of a very professional organization because it had to be at least as good as his food industry clients' cultures before they would respect the judging process and its outcome. Parker also had to upgrade the size of his staff—from a mere eight full-time people when he bought the company to the 53 chefs and 23 other staff people he now employs full time or outsources. He launched the ChefsBest Center for Taste in San Francisco, assembling a group of leading international experts on food including food technologists, flavorists, and even "psycho-sensory" analysts. With the help of these new professionals, American Culinary ChefsBest has recently added taste-testing of spirits including vodka and tequila. Every time Parker goes into a new area of the food business, the company has to develop a whole new judging process that withstands challenges so that each of the winners—and potential licensees—is assured of credibility and integrity from the company.

Third, Parker soon saw that he had to work hard to educate consumers about the company. Are consumers looking for the ChefsBest Award when they do their shopping at the grocery store? According to Parker, there are more than 40,000 products in the average grocery store. The larger grocery stores, like Ralph's or Safeway or Jewel, usually carry twice that number. When shoppers go in the supermarkets they are barraged by competing labels. In fact, Parker maintains that the average consumer is exposed to more than 4,000 advertising messages a day, so that when they arrive at the grocery store they're overwhelmed by the choices. "Our mission is to empower the consumer to make the very best buying decision possible, because we're the taste people. When consumers see the ChefsBest Award on products in the grocery store, they know they are buying the best-tasting product."

Now that Parker has the infrastructure and strategy in place and has managed to deal with the most troublesome issues he faced after buying the company, his big challenge now is generating broader consumer awareness of the ChefsBest award. Knowing Parker, that's another summit he will reach.

Organically Groomed

Parachuting CEOs like Parker, Streeter, and Zander are not the only kind of executives who bump into surprises during their first days and months on the job. Let us now turn our attention to an executive who came to his position "organically," having already been an insider.

Dave Vander Zanden, CEO, School Specialty. Although he had been with his company for more than three years as second-in-command, Dave Vander Zanden nevertheless found himself, at age 47, faced with an enormous surprise simply because of the nature in which he was thrust into his CEO job—suddenly and completely unexpectedly under difficult circumstances.

Authentic and unassuming, Vander Zanden is a down-to-earth guy but with a mind of his own and a vision that is tough and clear. He has fading blond hair and a middle-aged physique that in blue jeans, which he wore the day of our interview, looks more like a teenager's. Vander Zanden works in a simple "company issue" office, the same size and furnishing as the rest of the team's. He has no fear about not following the latest management fad. He keeps a strict open-door policy at his office. In fact, at School Specialty, a company that sells everything but the textbooks to educational institutions, it is rare that any office door is shut. One of the company legends is that his predecessor actually had the doors removed at a company School Specialty had acquired because its executive team kept shutting their office doors after paying lip service to their promise of keeping them—and in turn their communications—open to all their associates. What's more, Vander Zanden does not believe in the written performance review, and he guarantees you won't find one in the file of any School Specialty associate.

Vander Zanden was president and chief operating officer at School Specialty before he became CEO after the sudden death of Dan Spalding, the 47-year-old incumbent, his close friend and a leader he deeply admired. The relationship that he and Spalding had in managing the company was probably a lot different from what most CEOs have with their number two guy.

They met through the local YPO (Young Presidents' Organization) and formed a fast friendship. Vander Zanden was wrapping up an assignment for a family-owned company he had turned around. At the YPO meetings, Spalding mentioned that his organization was getting larger and he needed to get more help. Vander Zanden listened to that while at the same time he was telling the group that in a couple of years he'd be wrapping things up on his current job and needed to start thinking about what was next. Spalding and Vander Zanden started exploring the possibility of getting together on something.

At the time, School Specialty was a division of the burgeoning US Office Products Company. Vander Zanden made it clear he wasn't interested in ending up at the division level; he wanted to be at corporate. He believed that School Specialty was going to explode—it was just a question of when. Spalding called Vander Zanden in late 1997 and said that US Office Products was making some organizational changes, including the spin-off of School Specialty into a stand-alone company. Vander Zanden responded he was now ready to talk. Over the next few months, they crafted a deal: they would run the company like a partnership, with Spalding as CEO, taking Wall Street (investor and analyst relations) and acquisitions, and Vander Zanden taking the day-to-day business operations. And that's what they did—for about three and a half years.

In March 2002 Spalding and Vander Zanden, along with their families, went to an industry outing in Durango, Colorado, that included skiing. Spalding had always been a very big, strong skier. They used to call him the "Energizer bunny" because he'd constantly be up and down the hill. That's what he did—he just skied—and that was what he did that day too. When they were done, Vander Zanden picked him up in their car and asked how it went. He knew that Spalding—a five-mile-a-day runner—had experienced chest pains that year. A stent was put in his heart to correct a blockage. Yet Spalding started having some uncomfortable feelings from the stent. He still was having intermittent chest pains when the ski trip occurred. His doctors were trying to figure out what was going on. It was one of those things where it hurt today but then it was good for the next three weeks.

Spalding told Vander Zanden that he'd had a good day skiing, but that "he could feel it a little bit" and so had taken things easy. They all went to dinner and had a great time.

The next morning Vander Zanden awoke at 5:30 to the sound of a siren. Soon there was a knock on the front door and Vander Zanden went to Spalding's room. The story is still difficult for Vander Zanden to tell. Paramedics were in there working on Spalding and it didn't go well. Spalding technically died in his room. He had gotten out of bed with chest pains, took one step toward the bathroom, fell to the floor, and never got up.

Here was Vander Zanden, in the midst of the whole experience and his own horror, trying to comfort Spalding's wife. The first thing Vander Zanden felt he had to do was get word to the rest of Spalding's family. Next, he had to get both of the families in Colorado back home that day. He had to transport the body out of state, which meant he had to figure out what that entailed and get a funeral home to do something quickly.

He started working on all the unfamiliar personal and family issues associated with the tragic circumstances. Vander Zanden remembers that as they were getting all the family items done, he was on the phone, calling in to the office, talking to the CFO and saying that no one could be told anything. The market was open by then. It was about 10 A.M. in New York. He asked the CFO to call the board and convene a meeting for that morning. As soon as the CFO got them together, he was to get Vander Zanden on the phone so they could get a press release out to the market. They had the board meeting and decided what to do. They wanted to put some stability in place for the market so they appointed the board member with the most seniority as the interim chairman and Vander Zanden as interim CEO. As they got the message to the marketplace, they also had 2,500 associates to notify of what was going on.

He and the CFO started crafting something that they could get out to all the associates, to get the message to them and also give them some assurance that everything would be fine, that things would keep going. In the midst of all the other arrangements he was juggling, he and the CFO got notification out that same day. It was a Friday, which Vander Zanden believes turned out to be a bit of a blessing for them because it gave them two days to start to get things done.

As Vander Zanden tells it, "I knew what I had to do; I knew what was urgent, what I had to get done. I knew I had to get everybody reassured that the company is solid, the management team is in place. So while acknowledging that Dan had been our leader and was really loved by everybody—he was one of the best entrepreneurs I ever met in my life—at the same time, I had to assure everyone that we would go on without him, without skipping a beat."

Next he had a website set up where people could share their feelings about Spalding. "Everybody had funny stories about Dan and we said send them in. Take a minute and write down your experiences with this guy. We told people that if they had a personal relationship with Dan and needed to be away from the office, then do that. If they needed to be here or if they just needed to sit down and talk for a while with me or anyone, then that's what they should do. If it took a day or a week or a month—we told everyone to work their way through the grief the best way they could."

How did Vander Zanden take care of his own feelings? His close friend and closest work colleague has just died unexpectedly. He says that taking over the top role when someone that close to you passes away is tough to do, but you have to. From his perspective of the organization, there were a couple of hundred people who felt close to Spalding and the rest who thought of him simply as the CEO of the company. They lived across the country. They had seen his picture. So Vander Zanden took the position that he had to take care of the smaller core group, while at the same time, the company needed some leadership. He had stepped into the new role while figuring out how he was going to balance the organization's needs.

Then he had to balance his own feelings—his own grief. He trusted his gut to find the right spot and figure out what he needed to do.

"That was step one—we got the organization to understand that Dan did one great thing and he built a team that will keep it going. Our history says that's what we do," says Vander Zanden.

Luckily, Vander Zanden says, apart from the shock and surprise of the circumstances in which he had to become CEO, he's found nothing unexpected in the company itself since taking Spalding's place. His relationship with Spalding had been so close that they both knew "everything about everything." There wasn't anything about the company Vander Zanden didn't know, and, he maintains, "There hasn't been anything since Spalding's death that I have discovered and said, 'Gee, I didn't know about that.' Nothing little. Nothing big. We just told each other everything, all the time. I sat in this office. He sat in that office. We shared an assistant. We just ran the business together. We felt that if the two of us were consistent on the issues then the associates don't get confused about anything. Our philosophies were very similar as far as culture and respect for people."

◆ ◆ ◆

As the stories in this chapter illustrate, while it would be wonderful if an executive could step into a job facing no surprises—the reality is sometimes quite the opposite. But what about the next steps? Do even the best executives in a new position always have a solid plan—as the belief commonly holds—for making a sudden impact? That is the focus of the next chapter.

2

TO PLAN OR NOT TO PLAN?

Myth #2: High-impact executives walk into the job
with a solid game plan.

When Peter Dolan was appointed CEO of Bristol-Myers Squibb in
mid-2001, at age 44, little did he know that one of his first challenges would be dealing with a notorious stockholder in a company
in which Bristol-Myers Squibb had made sizable investments: none
other than Martha Stewart. What's more, his new position proved
to be far more consuming than he'd ever imagined. Dolan had been
a senior executive with the company for a number of years and was
used to working long hours to succeed. Yet he found his new job
was truly a 24 hours a day, seven days a week role. Over the span of
his twenty-year career, Dolan had always been able to compartmentalize his various roles. Becoming CEO changed that from the
moment his promotion was announced. He knew the job itself was
going to take up more of his life, especially in the beginning as he
learned the ropes, but he underestimated the pervasive public nature
of the job. As Dolan says, "As much as people tell you that's the case,
it's hard to fathom or appreciate until you're in the role."

For Dolan, the public nature of his job was further amplified by
Bristol-Myers Squibb's investment in ImClone. When Martha
Stewart got indicted for her sale of ImClone stock, the press was
beating down Dolan's door. He was barraged with questions around
the situation, most frequently: If Martha Stewart was selling
her stock to avoid losses and getting in hot water for it, why was
Bristol-Myers Squibb hanging on to its investment?

Dolan admits he did not have all the answers, nor could he
have a solid plan to deal with such a dire situation of uncontrol-
lable, swiftly unfolding revelations. He learned to rely on the advice

of his public relations people, to ignore the whole Stewart debacle as much as possible, and to keep focused one step at a time on the big picture of leading Bristol-Myers into the 21st century with a growing pipeline of innovative pharmaceutical solutions. As Dolan states, "We had made an investment in ImClone for its cancer drug, Erbitux. We had lots of people questioning that deal and why we made the investment that we did. There was an entire media circus created around the side issue [of Stewart] not related to the company investment but related to others who were famously involved in it. Ultimately the drug got approved. It's helping cancer patients. It's a strategic drug we needed for our oncology business. And, yes I do feel some level of vindication by the outcome."

As Dolan's story makes clear, great executives don't always step into a new job with a plan ready to execute—contrary to popular belief. In Dolan's case, any plan he might have made would have been quickly tabled, given the pressing situation demanding his attention.

An Outside Chance

Let's look now at a few more executives who, like Dolan, weren't necessarily able to craft a plan for what to do in the first days and months on the job. Not surprisingly, with a few exceptions, these executives have one important thing in common: they came to their jobs from outside the company.

What Plan?

"What kind of plan did I make to create change in the first 90–100 days?" CEO Dave Vander Zanden repeats. There's a period of time in a situation like this [the sudden death of Vander Zanden's predecessor] where you *don't change anything*, out of respect for the deceased and the grief everybody was going through. Any big changes came much later in the process because people had to get through the loss first."

Jamie Dimon, CEO, Bank One. When we left Jamie Dimon back in Chapter One, he was in the middle of a very *unwelcoming* first day as CEO of Bank One. Things did not get better for Dimon immediately, to say the least—and what's more, he did not know exactly what to do about it. Even for a leader of Dimon's mettle, he found it all just "really hard."

"It got me," he recalls about his situation. "It's not like you're at least with friends and people you know. You're all by yourself. There's nobody. Not even the secretary to talk to. Nothing."

Besides dealing with a difficult first day on the job, Dimon also had to figure out what to do about the fact that the company itself was in worse shape than Dimon had been led to believe. Bank One had extended too much credit and Dimon was astonished by how exposed they were. Expenses were also very bad. The company was out of control. Another thing that astounded him was the continued existence of multiple IT systems. To Dimon, it wasn't just the seven IT systems—it was the seven different companies, or at a minimum the four biggest acquisitions—that Bank One still fronted. Everything done in Kentucky or Texas or Chicago, for example, was different—different loan systems, different wire systems, different deposit systems, different statement systems, different teller systems—the whole thing. It became clear to him that it was killing his new organization.

Even with that realization, however, Dimon could not have *planned* what to do about all of this. In fact, Dimon is very outspoken about the folly of having a plan when you come into a new job, especially if you're from the outside. He just can't comprehend how you could have enough information ahead of time—and this view from a guy who grew up in the financial industry and did his homework about the new opportunity. Dimon had not been a CEO before, and he knew his background was stronger in certain areas of the bank than in others. Moreover, at Bank One, based in Chicago, he was stepping into a culture very different from his previous employer, Citibank, rooted on the East Coast. Dimon was a fast-talking New Yorker while all the various banking entities combined

What Plan?

Manpower International CEO Jeffrey Joerres says, "I still remember in my first 100 days I was thinking, I don't have my 100-day plan yet—I hope I'm not doing something wrong! Yet things felt good. That's one of those myths that just makes you wonder where it comes from."

into Bank One over the years came from gentler, kinder Midwestern or Southern roots.

As an outsider, he says, there was *no way* he could know beforehand what he would need to do to succeed. Once on the job, however, his approach was to gather as much information as he could put his hands on. Like Ed Zander, Dimon labeled his approach to his early days as "immersion." When asked whether he thought there were standards a new CEO should absolutely adopt, he replied: "There are not. There are some principles that I think you can follow in anything but you really have to get a feel for what is there, the people you are judging. Whatever prior judgments you have, you have to throw them out. Get rid of your preconceived notions. Do it full time—breakfast, lunch, dinner, every night. Read stacks of stuff, start meeting with people, start regular reviews, and tell people when you want to know something, and when you don't." It clearly worked for Dimon, who became CEO of JP Morgan Chase after that company acquired Bank One.

"Start town halls," Dimon continues. "Get issues raised, get traveling, go to different places. That whole time you're starting to get a feel for what the people are really like. On top of that, there's stuff you need to start now. Then there's the stuff for next quarter."

The one-step-at-a-time approach seemed to work well for Dimon. Soon he figured out that he had to reduce headcount by 10,000 people. He says, "You're not walking into meetings that are all joyous. Every town hall you have, you're asked, 'Are you closing us down?' I was very honest with people. I said, 'I'm going to tell you

what we know when we know it and I'm not going to lie to anyone.'
I said the same thing to shareholders, the mayor, and the governor.
You work really hard to make sure you have covered all your
bases—and then you have the board. I knew a lot of the action we
needed to take but there were some on the board who were reluctant. I had never managed a board before."

To resolve the problem of multiple IT systems, Dimon went on
the road and visited the bank's call centers. He'd see people answering the phone with three manuals on their desk—for instance,
Texas, the local area, and Illinois. He'd listen to the calls and see
the same problem over and over again. The bank's customer service
rep would pick up the phone and say, "Oh hello. Could you tell me
what state you're in?" That was so she could pick the right manual
and system. On top of that, each system had a different pass code
that had to be entered every time to gain access. Sometimes all of
the information was on one screen. Sometimes it wasn't. It was a
disaster for employee morale and for customer satisfaction.

Dimon discovered turnover was terrible as a result of the morale
problem. People had to be trained on at least three systems, and
even such things as interest rate calculations might be different on
each system. Much to his continued surprise and chagrin, Dimon
learned that the same type of fee at one branch might be $21 while
it was $24 at another branch—even though they both now had the
same name and might be handled by one call center. He wanted all
of the data to terminate into one of the systems and he was ada-
mant about it—whatever it took.

Dimon continued to uncover new challenges. The company
didn't have reports: no daily, weekly, monthly risk or credit reports.
They didn't have P&L's at the branch level. They had enormous
commercial credit burden—things were "way out of whack,"
according to Dimon. On top of that, the bank didn't have enough
reserves if they needed to write off assets. Dimon toughed it out, formulating more plans about what needed to get done than he had
ever anticipated. Sudden impact was a daily event as he was making critical decisions with far-reaching consequences.

Pat Russo, CEO, Lucent Technologies. When she stepped into her new job as CEO of Lucent Technologies, at age 49, Pat Russo bumped straight into an unexpectedly dismal market. Russo might be considered a hybrid—an "inside" outsider. She had left Lucent a mere 18 months previously for the COO job at Kodak. Coming back to Lucent, a leading developer and manufacturer of high-speed data and voice communications equipment, she assumed she could hit the ground running. If she had a "plan" before returning to Lucent, she would say she hoped to take the recently completed strategy work undertaken by a former CEO (Henry Schacht, who was her mentor), set her own priorities from the work, and develop a checklist of items to accomplish in the first 30, 60, and 90 days.

For Russo, an action-oriented executive with a résumé full of ground-breaking accomplishments, this might have been a relatively easy task under normal circumstances. She not only knew the people, she'd been part of the founding team when Lucent, formerly the Bell Labs and Western Electric divisions of AT&T, was spun off from Ma Bell. If anyone knew a company inside out going into a CEO role from the outside, it was Russo. Given her history with the company, she charged in believing that her personal priority was to execute on a strategy that had already been crafted by a group of great minds that she knew and respected.

In its early days, Lucent was the beneficiary of a sky-rocketing telecom market boom. Unknown to her at the time of accepting the CEO job, the company was on the edge of a bubble that was about to burst. As Russo explains, the unexpectedly incredible rate of market growth in the beginning was paralleled only by the unexpectedly incredible rate of market drop as she began her tenure. She and her team kept revising their plans downward expecting they had hit the bottom of the trough in the market, only to find it kept getting even worse. The industry analysts expected that the industry would be down by 5% going into 2002. The plan she expected to execute for the year had taken into account the analysts' pessimistic predictions and had a reasonable target of $17 billion in annual revenues. Going into the year, the Lucent team thought it was doable. Russo confirms that no one remembers any raised eyebrows over unreachable forecasts from the investment community, either.

As her first 100 days came to a close, the company was on a steep downward plunge. She shelved the strategy she'd planned to execute. Lucent ended the year at $12 billion in revenues rather than the $17 billion they—and most everyone else—had thought was achievable at the beginning of the year. As Russo said, "The year 2002 was a disaster. Spending in North America dropped 50% in the wireline business, which was unanticipated, not predictable, and unprecedented. . . . The depth and duration of the decline that ensued in the industry were well beyond what anybody in their wildest dreams could have imagined. I expected that I would be coming in and working to accelerate the strategy and make it better, that I'd be taking a set of good work that had been done and do better."

But, as Russo puts it, "Frankly, all hell broke loose! Even within the industry, nobody knew what the market did until after it happened. Everybody was adjusting their numbers through the year as they took a look at capital spending in the quarter. Gosh, it's down X—and there were always the views that it wasn't going to be as bad as it ultimately turned out to be. If you look at Lucent as a company and what we had to manage through—in our peak year in comparable business let's say—we probably had revenue in the $6 billion range—and we went down to $2 billion. You can't take costs down fast enough when your revenue is dropping like a rock, and that's what we experienced in 2002.

"Think about what had happened. The balance sheet had been worked with respect to getting more capital into the company. So we ended up having to do two convertible debt offerings, to shore up cash to weather the storm. The covenants on our credit lines ended up becoming questionable because of what was happening. We ended up operating without a credit line. Our credit rating was downgraded. So we had a number of capital market, financial balance sheet–related issues going on because of what was happening in the market."

Russo had a market that was absolutely unable to be planned for or determined—much less to have an instinct for what to do about it. She says that rather than planning, they were cycling through resizings and resizings believing that the market was leveling off and then bang—another new downturn would hit the industry. She says that at some point, her team, the industry, and even the Wall Street crowd were getting shell-shocked. They kept thinking another downturn wasn't possible. Russo was focused on the cost side. Her team was reducing people, cutting expenses, and doing everything else they could to lower costs and improve their bottom line. Yet the dilemma for Russo and her team was that with the nosedive in the market, they did not have control of top line revenue. Russo says that what they ended up doing (as opposed to what she thought they would be doing—enhancing strategy and doing even better) was shifting their mind-set very quickly to Job One, which was they absolutely had to weather the storm. She developed a steely resolve to do so because its depth and duration were unanticipated and could wreak absolute havoc across the company.

Russo's coping strategy in this market environment was to get very focused on the things she and her team could control. She had to make changes—a lot of changes: strategic changes, operating model changes, size and structure changes, and leadership changes as she went through figuring out how they were going to get out of it. It's an understatement to say that 2002, her first year as CEO, was very challenging. She dealt with every financial issue imaginable. Do you have enough liquidity to weather the storm? How much cash do you have? What do you do if it gets worse? How low can it go? Are your plans adequate? Are they not adequate? Plus, she and her team had to worry about their external stakeholders and the financial requirements to keep the business going—credit ratings, credit facilities, access to capital.

At the same time, the stock price—one of the key indicators to the investment community—was plummeting. In October 2002

Lucent dropped to 56–57 cents and its closest competitor, Nortel, had dropped to 44 cents. The financial community was questioning whether the industry was going to make it or not. There was concern that Lucent and others were going to run out of cash. Lucent faced the potential of being delisted from the NYSE, and Russo and her team had to find a cure for that. As Russo says, "Can you imagine? Now we can—but then, could you have *planned* for it?"

What Plan?

"If somebody had said to me when I became CEO of Lucent in January 2002, 'OK, Pat Russo, I've got a crystal ball, and it says your market soon is going to be cut in half, you're going to have to make massive cost reductions in this business, and you're going to have to do some capital market offers because you're going to burn through cash'—I wouldn't have believed them.

"But then I would have said, 'OK, now let me think about how I'm going to deal with that.' The problem is that so much of what we managed through in my first 12 to 24 months was happening *to* us. At the time, everyone believed the industry growth would just continue and a lot of folks got it wrong. *Nobody* saw this coming. It couldn't be planned for. I've had to do a lot of reaching for combinations of solutions and alternatives, brainstorming with key folks around me. I've had to do a lot of improvising."

Russo prevailed. By the end of 2003, Lucent again reported a quarterly profit, with dramatically improved margins and working capital requirements. Although Russo is a Yankee with a tough side, the Russo I met has been softened by the battering she took in the early months of her tenure. Having weathered the storm, she might be best described as a steel magnolia. She is still the polished, immaculately groomed, in-control executive, yet the glimmer in her eye and her candor when recounting experiences exude a certain humanness that has bloomed from adversity and uncertainty.

Jay Amato, CEO, Viewpoint. When Jay Amato was brought in as CEO of Viewpoint at age 44, he needed to turn the company around fast.[1] The 15-year-old software company had lost $215 million since its inception, was shrinking from a revenue perspective, and was losing $5–6 million a quarter. "In a small company in crisis, you don't do much long-term planning. You come up with it on Monday and you do it on Wednesday. It's like, Whistle me a few bars and then I'll sing along."

Amato said that finding the cash flow was always a problem in the beginning. He didn't know for a fact that a lot of his ideas would work. As he recalls, he and his team would be making changes and improvising as they went, while trying to keep people focused.

The best example of his own successful improvisation? He says it was obtaining a $10 million perpetual license fee from AOL instead of adding debt to the balance sheet. One day he was brainstorming about ways to raise cash without having to go to the banks for more money and without any new revenue streams on the horizon. He looked at what other options were available and figured out that if he were to offer a one-time payment for a perpetual license to AOL, it would save them money in the long run and up front give Viewpoint the cash that it desperately needed.

Amato, a guy who is always pushing the envelope and has never grasped the concept of political correctness over conviction, says that like a battle-scarred veteran, he's learned to trust his gut. He improvised, based on everything he learned from his previous company, Vanstar, and before. Now he has more real-time data, so his gut is much more supported because more information is available. New leaders have to be able to get the information in a way that allows them to take action and have an impact. The good news, he says, is that even small companies now have the tools to get that information and to access it more quickly.

Dick Notebaert, CEO, Qwest. When the incumbent CEO is not told that he is out of the job until the day you arrive, that makes it tough to come in with a concise game plan. As Dick Notebaert recounts about his first days at Qwest, the telecommunications company, "My predecessor wasn't informed until the last minute that he was being replaced, so I couldn't really get the in-depth information I needed walking in. You can do your homework, but unless you are coming in under a normal transition, you don't have the opportunity to do the type of research needed. All I could do was go to the website, talk to board members, and look at published financials. I couldn't very well come in here and interview the chief financial officer or go out to the garage and talk to the technicians, much less talk to customers."

Notebaert, who became Qwest's CEO at age 58, is a bundle of energy with piercing brown eyes and an impish grin. He's the kind of person who seems to sit on the edge of his chair, ready to spring into action. And that's exactly what he would have to do at Qwest if he hoped to resolve its problems. In fact, not long after Notebaert took the helm he saw that the company was in serious financial trouble with creditors—requiring new negotiations. This was definitely a case where any plan he might have had coming into the job would have had to be quickly scrapped, given the direness of the situation.

The company at that time did not have the ability to balance its cash account with any degree of accuracy and the variance was up to $100 million. Qwest needed to sell an asset, so the company

One Plan You *Should* Have

"There are a lot of people who insist on getting on your calendar when you become CEO," says Andrew Liveris of Dow Chemical. "One who will not be doing that is your customer. You need to know your customers. That's one plan you should have. They are the ones who buy your stuff. It's up to the CEO to get customers on the calendar. That's why I visited our top 50 customers during the time I was COO and am still regularly visiting customers and insisting that the people who report to me do the same."

sold what Notebaert and his CFO considered one of its less strategic assets, its directory business, Dex, for $7.05 billion. In return, Qwest received a paydown of $10 billion in debt. It was the largest bond exchange in the history of the country. Notebaert explains, "We said, you take a billion of the new bond and you give us a billion of the old bond back. So we were able to do exchanges. It was huge. It was several billion dollars and had never been done on that scale. We had the sale of Dex far enough along that we were able to go to some people and borrow $750 million at a high interest rate, and that resolved our insolvency which got us through 2002. Otherwise, we would not have been bankrupt. We would have been insolvent. Big difference."

But there were other things at Qwest that the new CEO hadn't planned on having to confront. From the start, he had to deal with abysmal employee morale. How bad was it? Technicians were so embarrassed about where they worked that they wouldn't wear their company-logo shirts or jackets on their way to and from work. Service at Qwest was notoriously bad, and they didn't want to be identified with the company. They got tired of all the disparaging remarks. The company's poor reputation was further sullied by the previous leadership's decision to end its long-standing tradition of supporting local community affairs.

Notebaert set out to craft a complete cultural transformation. "We had to restore credibility by providing outstanding service, and we had to motivate people to believe they work for the finest company in America." That transformation began in Notebaert's mind with a painting in his office of a telephone lineman, Angus MacDowell, trudging through the blizzard of 1888 to inspect overhead phone lines and make sure his customers stayed connected. He explains, "That painting conveyed, 'No matter what happens, I'll be there for you.' It was titled 'The Spirit of Service,' and that phrase—plus that commitment—became the bedrock of Qwest's transformation."

At the outset, Notebaert put a number of stakes in the ground. He and the rest of the top team would communicate often—and with transparency. They would flatten hierarchy. They'd do everything they said they would do. They would put all their efforts on a fast track—if experts said it takes five to seven years to transform a culture, they would do it in two or three.

Notebaert knows while that work will never be done, transformation has taken place. It has renewed Qwest people. It has also benefited Qwest customers. While customer loyalty for the telecom industry overall, as measured by the University of Michigan's American Customer Satisfaction Index, dropped since last year's survey, Qwest advanced nine points—a best-in-class improvement for a single year. The company has already heard from one of its three counterparts—those being SBC, Verizon, and BellSouth—asking to benchmark how it achieved those results.

Just for the record, Notebaert says, "Our techs aren't the only ones wearing Qwest-branded clothing these days. We all wear it. Everywhere we go. In 2003, the first full year the Spirit of Service was in place, Qwest people spent more than a million dollars of their own money to buy shirts, sweaters, and other items sporting the Qwest logo. And that kind of pride continues. Last month alone, employees spent another $137,000."

On the financial front, Qwest restated earnings, settled with the SEC, and reduced debt by more than $10 billion. "In three years, we straightened all that out. When I got here we had just over $26 billion in debt. Today we have about $17 billion and we have about $2.5 billion in cash on hand. That means—subtracting those items—our net debt is below $15 billion, which is where US West was before the merger. So financially, we still have work to do. We need to get it down to around $11–12 billion. But we're doing it."

Notebaert feels a mark of the financial community's confidence was when lenders proactively aligned with the Qwest team in their highly publicized pursuit of MCI last year. As of mid-2005, on the last quarterly earnings report, he was able to tell analysts that Qwest was the only wire-line carrier in the nation to have improved margins over the last five quarters. Not bad for a CEO who didn't come in with a preconceived plan to deal with these corporate conundrums.

Notebaert adds that in his job, he has had to improvise every day. "Do we have this infrastructure? No. Are we able to find our way around it? Sure, absolutely. That's the kind of improvising you have to do every day, but in a very disciplined way. Discipline is critical in the process. There is no need to panic, no need to be hectic, no need to knee-jerk. You have to be methodical, disciplined. But that doesn't mean long cycle times. Short cycle times can be accomplished if you're disciplined and methodical vs. knee-jerk. Said another way: Stay on message. You can't have a flavor of the month."

Stephanie Burns, CEO, Dow-Corning.   For Stephanie Burns, a self-described Dow-Corning "lifer" who became CEO of the company at age 48, her ability to plan was most challenged at an earlier point in her career, when she headed the company's internal health care business. Her business unit made silicone-based materials for health care product manufacturers. One of her unit's customers was Wright Orthopedics, a company Dow-Corning had recently acquired. Wright used these materials for joint replacements and breast implants.

Unbeknownst to Burns or the company, she assumed her position in the midst of the growing nationwide—and unsubstantiated—innuendo around the health and safety of silicone breast implants. The fear would surge into a tide of inquiries and accusations from ad hoc special interest groups, government agencies, and women's organizations across the country.

Talk about being unable to make a plan on the new job! Burns had hardly gotten her footing as head of the business when she was flung into this brewing controversy. With the advent of the crisis, Burns' assignment turned into Director of Women's Health, and she was made part of a small "tiger team" in the company formed specifically to deal with the issue.

Burns, a leader who is warm and authentic—with an underlying passion for the business to which she has devoted her entire career—took it on herself to reach out to women's groups during the crisis. This included women's research organizations, breast cancer groups, and the Society for Women's Health Research, a Washington-based watchdog organization that ensures, rather than funds, the inclusion of women in health studies. In her new role, Burns also served as the interface with the FDA at a time when Dow-Corning's relationship with the agency was very strained. The FDA had just recommended not approving continued marketing of breast implants. Burns' mission for the next four years was to build Dow-Corning's credibility, cite science as the grounds for decision making, and bring attention to ongoing research. The company funded $40 million in further research on breast implants. Along the way, Burns not only got to know external stakeholders but got to know many of the stars inside the company as she sought information and support.

Burns says the affair was a long, drawn-out chain of fear-mongering that started with accusations that breast implants cause cancer. After no hard evidence was found, detractors moved on to another list of diseases to which they tried to link implants. Subsequently, scientific panel and judge panel rulings have vindicated Dow-Corning. Burns says that the positive outcome of the experience is Dow-Corning's enhanced relationship with the FDA. (Dow-Corning has since sold the device business, though it still supplies silicone to breast implant manufacturers.) As a result of her leadership during the crisis, Burns was appointed executive vice president—putting her on the inside track for CEO, which she attained in July 2004.

"I really sympathized with the women who were so frightened," Burns says, "especially when there was no reason for the scare. But I felt good about the whole outcome and how the company handled the controversy."

◆　◆　◆

As shown in this chapter, high-impact executives do *not* necessarily always come into the job with a solid plan for sudden impact.

Most relied on hard facts and information that they painstakingly gathered. Others had no choice but to simply ride the wave of what was occurring and to wait to see how things unfolded before making definitive decisions.

Let us turn now to another common myth that surrounds new leaders: that they should wait and get to know their teams before making any changes.

3

REACH FOR THE STARS

Myth #3: High-impact executives play it safe
and get to know their new teams before making
changes.

When Jay Amato became CEO of Viewpoint, he walked into a
company truly in crisis. As he began to devise solutions in the early
weeks, he became increasingly frustrated with the existing management team and their nay-saying. To every idea he proposed,
someone replied, "Oh we tried that—it didn't work." He brought
up the idea of using their own distribution list to introduce new
products, and everybody said, "Oh, no, we can never do that. That
would be terrible. People would be very upset if we start prompting
them for updates or upgrades or anything of that nature, even if it
was free." (Amato's idea ended up generating much-needed revenue—although it did cost him some customer goodwill.)

As Amato recalls, "Honestly, after about two weeks, you could
tell the people who were spending all of their time justifying why
things were bad vs. the ones who were trying to figure out, based on
my crazy idea of turning things upside down, ways to make it possible." Amato found it helpful to talk to middle managers, the people
who make the day-to-day company run. As usual, they had a very
good idea of who was pulling their weight and who was "hiding in
the corner" hoping nobody was going to find them.

Within two weeks on the job, Amato fired 14 of the 22 executives at VP level or above. He felt he had to take a contrarian position because the company was at a point where it could not worry
about whether a couple of people were going to be upset about it or
not. It was fighting for its very existence. He insisted that team
members find a way to get the company back on its feet and change
their attitudes to focus on what could be done, not what couldn't.

"Let me tell you something. Of all the things I have done in this company that have brought me credibility with the employees, the people here were astounded at how I surgically removed those 14 executives. At the end of the day there wasn't one of those 14 people that anybody said we shouldn't have fired. Those people were cumbersome. There was a lot of job duplication, costing the company extra money and causing it to move much slower than it needed to because they created an environment of politics that a company this size just couldn't live with."

One reason this had happened was that—as is often the case—the previous CEO suffered from the history issue. His history with the 14 executives made it nearly impossible for him to fire anyone. Amato underscores "paralysis by history," remembering that when he arrived, there were three CFOs—two exes and one new one. They all had different jobs and unfortunately, even with three of them, none had put Viewpoint in the position of having high-quality management reporting and controls.

The additional advantage for the company was that by eliminating those executives, Amato got rid of 14 high-end salaries rather than the 40 lower salaries it would have required to achieve the same positive financial effect. Another positive impact of the early firing: "It uncovered a lot of jewels in the company—people in the company that are really superstars, who since 18–20 months ago have really risen to the occasion. They helped us build the new products and features that are really driving our success with the new growth."

Clearly Amato made a sudden impact when it came to ridding his firm of fading stars. Contrary to the common wisdom to "play it safe" and take time before doing any radical surgery or getting in a new team, Amato and many of the CEOs I interviewed adhere to what I call the Nike plan: "Just do it." And, these CEOs would add, "do it faster or better than anyone else."

Better means, of course, surrounding yourself with the best people you can find. Whether you are a CEO or in another leadership position, you are only one person. It is impossible to know everything, hear everything, or be everywhere. The people you surround yourself with are the best prevention of and, when necessary, recovery from mistakes.

But how do you find those people? How do you reach for the star players for your team? Just because the previous CEO failed, does it mean that every member of the team also failed? The question usually means looking first to the team you just inherited from the old regime—and in fact, later in this chapter I'll present some examples of people who did just that. But for the most part, the CEOs I spoke with disagreed with conventional wisdom.

Find Your Team Fast

Let's look at a few more executives who took the same approach that Amato did: When it came to getting a team in place, they found that faster is better. But the issue of how quickly new executives move ignores the question of how they came into their roles in the first place. Does the fact that executives were insiders rather than outsiders (or vice versa) have any impact on how they reached for their stars?

Peter Dolan, CEO, Bristol-Myers Squibb. Although he'd been with the company more than a decade when he was promoted to COO, Dolan feels he doesn't quite fit the "insider" label since he'd had little experience with the pharmaceutical side of the business. He said that the insider/outsider distinction of his career is important because he had many instances within his company where he was new to the situation and had to make swift judgments about who his stars were in order to achieve sudden impact.

For example, when Dolan joined Mead-Johnson in 1995, he had to make some quick decisions about the senior members of the team, and he made those decisions within weeks. Then in his tenure at Zimmer, another of the company's entities, he made the decision that many of the senior people there probably were not the stars to take the company forward. While he was only with the business for one year, Dolan installed a new chief for Europe, recruited a new president from the outside, and appointed a new head of marketing. In the process, he developed a sense of getting the right people in place—and doing it fast. As he puts it: "Get the right people and your own people in place *as soon as possible*. At this level, people are very competent. Not only must they be competent, they must be committed 110% to your agenda."

Dolan said it's key to have a clear delineation of when someone is really in charge. When Dolan became CEO, some of those who would become his team members had been promoted by the former CEO at the same time. With the simultaneous movement of these people, Dolan had limited ability to reach for his own stars. As a result, Dolan has two teams. One is his direct reports, which number nine, and the other an expanded group, the Executive Committee, which has 13 members and meets less frequently.

Probably the most significant impact he feels he has had would be aligning the organization behind a strategy and plan in the midst of what he characterized as a hurricane of both internal and external events at Bristol-Myers Squibb in 2002, the year he became CEO. He took an organization whose morale was down, whose members were questioning whether the company had a strategy—and within 18 months—built exceptional alignment within the organization, not only at the top but throughout. He did this, clearly, because he had a good team around him, which he had put in place immediately.

Jeffrey Joerres, CEO, Manpower. Joerres took the helm at Manpower at age 38, having risen in the company organically. He didn't need advice about finding rising stars or determining who was trustworthy, because he already had on-the-job knowledge built in his prior roles in the company. His biggest issue wasn't finding the rising stars but dealing with some of the supposed stars on his executive team and in other key roles.

Joerres, who is smart, shrewd, and driven yet uncannily retains his enthusiastic, wholesome hometown boy image, recalls he had a dysfunctional group of people thinking only about themselves. He was able to choose his closest allies carefully because of his prior experience in the organization. While he kept most of the executives in place when he was promoted, most are in different jobs now. Joerres used a surgical approach in changing his team. He had two key people who wanted to retire when he was promoted. The head of Manpower France had been there 40 years—he had run France longer than Joerres had been alive. The head of U.S. operations had been with Manpower for 27 years. Joerres did not want to replace both of them at the same time. As Joerres says, "There are only so many variables that you can have going on at one time and still be successful. Changing leadership in our two largest operations at once was not the best scenario."

He separated the retirements by asking the U.S. leader to stay on longer so both did not happen at the same time. They were very important positions and he wanted time to think it through. In Joerres' own words, "I don't want it to be like that science experiment where you don't know what change caused what outcome because everything's mixed up in the beaker at the same time." Joerres selected an inside star for Europe and brought in someone from the outside for the United States. Financial results at the end of Joerres' first year in office demonstrated that his strategy worked—net income grew 13% on sales growth of 9% and earnings per share had increased a whopping 19%. In subsequent years, *Fortune* magazine has named Manpower the best company to work for in its industry category.

Pat Russo, CEO, Lucent Technologies. Russo doesn't feel she quite fits as an "outsider" either, even though I presented her technically as such in Chapter Two, because she spent so many years of her career at Lucent and was only gone for 18 months. Upon returning to Lucent to take the helm, Russo had the challenge of reaching for the stars while also needing to eliminate a few of the established stars of the troubled company. One of the first things she did was remove one of the senior levels of the company—the COO position—so she could get closer to the business. She changed Lucent's operating model. She didn't hesitate to go to the outside to find talent as needed. She created a global sales head and brought in an outside individual for that. She created a chief marketing officer position and did the same. She brought in a new head of IT. With these appointments, Russo strategically reached for three stars early on from the outside and made an immediate impact on the organization. She recently made more significant changes by bringing in a new chief strategy officer, a new general counsel, and a new head of Bell Laboratories, the renowned research arm of AT&T that became part of Lucent at divestiture. Russo has made a lot of changes to the team. She initiated the changes from the outside when she determined that she needed a new model or fresh eyes; the business required a different experience set.

As far as how Russo deals with the schmoozers vs. the real stars, she says she knows there is a certain amount of that but you can get wise to it pretty quickly. It's another advantage of not having a history. She recalls in her previous position as COO at Kodak, where she was an outsider, she made a very significant change in the organizational structure that affected a good guy but she believed it was the right thing to do for the business and it had to be done. Nobody had been willing to pick it up because of their common history. She looked at the situation and said it didn't make sense. People there did not want to deal with it, while Russo, without the history, was saying, What's the big deal? She did it with care, but she had to do it. She knew it was something others weren't prepared to do. She has seen that when people are together for a long time, there is more tolerance. As Russo aptly said, "History has a way of creating its own legends."

As for identifying the stars at Lucent, Russo already knew many people in the company because of her previous tenure there. She had the benefit of the history and the relationships. She had the benefit of knowing the reputations of people and their ability to develop talent and she found all that to be helpful.

In Russo's mind, having a history can be an advantage but she feels not having a history when stepping into a new company has advantages too. There are no loyalties. You have rational emotion and intellect in your favor. There is some freshness that is an advantage. The disadvantages are you don't know where the bodies are buried and you don't know who you can count on right away. That has to be built.

When Slower Is Better

Let's look now at executives who took a different tack when it came to getting their teams in place. These CEOs didn't rush the process; rather, they believed it was crucial to take time if they hoped to end up with the best possible team. We begin with Motorola's Ed Zander who, unlike Pat Russo, came to his company fresh, unattached to anyone in the organization or on his team.

Ed Zander, CEO, Motorola. When Zander took charge at Motorola after many years at Sun Microsystems, his outsider perspective had a definite impact on the people he chose to be on his team and how he chose them. He told everybody that he was going to measure them over six to nine months. He gave everyone a clean slate for the first six months. Then, one morning in June (he had arrived in January) he remembers waking up and deciding it was time to make some changes on the team. Surprisingly, as an outsider, he stuck mainly with insiders. Zander says there have been three additions and a promotion to his team, a total of four changes.

Four weeks after Zander joined Motorola, the company had a great quarter after two really weak quarters that had propelled his predecessor's departure. Zander says the positive results made it harder for him to make changes and almost worked against him. As he said, "When you come in to maybe an IBM at the time Gerstner did, or during a real turnaround, you get a chance to just slash and burn overnight. When you've had a great first quarter, you say to

Why I Kept the Old Regime's Team

When Irene Rosenfeld took the helm at Frito-Lay, she made a decision not many new CEOs do: she kept the existing team. Why? Because with a few exceptions, Frito-Lay was in tip-top shape. While she could see a need for the culture to change, the company had no major financial problems, so she didn't have the mandate for fast change that accompanies financial deterioration. She says that the few new team members were almost entirely promotions from within the company. Rather than advocating wholesale change, Rosenfeld recruited one new person who had a unique set of skills who has been able to accelerate some of the changes she was looking for.

For a whole variety of reasons, Rosenfeld thinks it can be difficult when the CEO brings in a whole new regime. Frito-Lay, for example, is a tightly integrated culture and most everyone who is there has been there for many years. "They all know each other," Rosenfeld says. "They go to church together. You have to be really careful when you start plucking people out of that kind of an environment."

yourself, maybe this team just needs leadership. Sometimes—like we've seen in baseball and football and sports, you get a new manager or leader of the same players and you get incredible performance out of them. So you have to be careful, you have to say, does this team just need new leadership to improve performance?" The quandary for Zander involved deciding if he really had the stars or not. Had they just had the wrong director or did he need new actors in the roles?

Zander saw the positive change firsthand that occurred when he brought in a new leader—an insider—in one of the divisions. "We appointed Ron Garriques in September to be president of the mobile devices business, and it's been like night and day. Same team. Same style. He's just got leadership characteristics and the know-how to get more out of a team." Zander brought him in from Motorola's European business. He gave an outside search firm the assignment first and, as he puts it, interviewed everybody in the country. Garriques beat them all. It was a very open process.

Zander ultimately brought in a few outsiders but first worked to find the stars internally. He felt that as he and the top team looked at the second ranks they saw where some of the issues were and started to "sprinkle in some new vice presidents." When they reconstituted the organization, about four more people were affected. Some of them exited and some went into different jobs. Zander made it clear he wanted a different team at the table. His senior leadership team today is down from 17 to about a dozen— and of those, at most five are outsiders. Zander subscribes to a policy that he calls "a third, a third, a third"—a third promote, a third stay, and a third new. He felt he just had to get the leadership and team working in tandem. Instead of a wholesale change-out of the team, Zander focused on new leaders and new scripts for the fastest impact.

As for who he brought onto this team, he says: "I'm not the kind of guy who would come in and say, 'All my career I was at Sun, so I'm going to quickly bring in twelve of my Sun friends.' Some people do that, and I'm not saying it's wrong. There are friends who probably wanted to come. There were one or two I did want to get but they didn't want to move to the Midwest."

Jamie Dimon, CEO, Bank One. Unlike Zander, when Jamie Dimon took the helm at Bank One, he *did* want to hire friends whom he trusted and with whom he had a history. His biggest challenge was the noncompete contract he'd signed with his former employer, which precluded his direct recruitment of former allies.

Still, Dimon shared Zander's method of taking time to select his team. "There are certain decisions that you have to do right, not fast," he says. "Especially people decisions. If you make a mistake on those, you pay six months, twelve months. It takes you a long time to figure it out and a long time to replace them. If you make the right decision with people (especially the leaders)—boom!—that whole unit's going to come into its own. They'll do anything. So you have to be very careful about people decisions."

So get to know people, but set your priorities. Dimon explained that if he knew certain people decisions weren't going to affect the company's stock and he knew he had to do it, he just did it. His instinct was that he wasn't taking that much risk. It was better than what he had or from his perspective, at a minimum, it would surface what he had. Other places, he couldn't do that—it was too much risk. For instance, he couldn't afford to have someone who couldn't do the job in the vital capital markets trading area. Dimon knew someone he respected in that area and brought him in.

Dimon developed a practical way to identify stars internally. His method was to find one star who could then advise on the entire constellation of potential high-performers. He said finding the stars is almost impossible by yourself. For him, it was accomplished through a lot of evenings of cocktails and dinner. Dimon grins, "You're taking people out for cocktails constantly. And then when you find out who's good, it gets exponential. If I met you and I found out you were good, I'd ask you. What about this? What about that? What do you think about them? It put me in a position where now I had you being helpful too. It got even better when I hired outside people with whom I had done a lot of turnarounds. Usually we'd wait until there were four or five of us so we could forge and have a certain amount of camaraderie. Someone might say, 'What did you think of John?' And I might say well I feel the same or differently but we'd listen to each other. We'd help each see who was good, who was not good."

How did he deal with the schmoozers? "I always say the bull-shitters are pretty good. They've been practicing it for 25 years. There were a lot of bullshitters in this company. Eventually you can figure it out. You don't have to decide right away. Give yourself six weeks, eight weeks, ten weeks, but after a while you know. Honestly, the odds are they know already too. There's a good amount of book on everyone." He feels reaching for the right stars and getting it right from the start is critical: "You don't want to make people mistakes. You have to deal with them constantly and intensively."

Dimon is an incessant questioner. When he wanted to test if someone knew the business, he'd ask a lot of questions: "What about this? What about that? How can we do this? What about the competition? What does Citi do in this situation? What does Wachovia do? How would you compensate for this?" After a while Dimon could detect who didn't know the business—at all. As Dimon says, "It was completely honest and it wasn't just the bullshitters, it was the incompetents. There were a lot of those. It's clear after a while. You'd say, you work in this position, so why are there three different account plans for branch managers? They would babble on and I'd ask, 'What other one did we look at?' They'd say we did one based on profits and one based on sales and I'd ask, 'How do you measure sales? Describe the one you did. How do you report profits?' And they don't know." Dimon wasn't afraid to put people on the hot seat to achieve fast impact.

Dimon can't stress enough the importance of having excellent people on the team. And a can-do attitude mixed with savvy experience is the key. Dimon advises carefully selecting your team without being intimidated by those who are left behind. "Make sure you have good people with you—the right types of people. That's not so simple having said it. You have a lot of people who are saying, 'What do you mean, why them, why not me?' And you say, 'Look at where we are.' These are the very same crummy people that got us there in the first place. Very few are willing to move on or give in to change. It's a terrible situation. The bullshitters will bullshit you too and all of a sudden you are where you were before." Thus Dimon learned firsthand what Russo earlier referred to as the "history problem" that breeds retention of incompetents.

Dimon called people outside the company about people. He creatively sought information from a lot of different places. One way Dimon figured out who his stars were was through outside consultants who had worked for Bank One prior to his tenure. Dimon learned that the consultants knew a lot of his team from past engagements. He'd call and find out what they thought about certain people. Dimon also learned about people from the company's outside legal counsel. "If you looked at my calendar back then, I'd be seeing a lot of lawyers who did work for people here. Once I found out that they used so-and-so lawyer, I'd pick up the phone and say give me a real evaluation. They know that I'm going to run the company so they wouldn't bullshit me on that. Give me an evaluation of A, B, and C. Why did the company do these certain things? What do you think of the people? So from consultants to lawyers, sometimes even investment bankers, you get a lot of feedback."

Today Dimon is applying much of his experience to JP Morgan Chase, where after a short stint as president he was appointed CEO. Like raising your second child after a first difficult one, he says, the experience of leadership does get easier, better. "Some of the things that seemed big diminish over time. You get better focused on what matters. What's most important is to get the right person in the right job. Get them in the right job and it's a grand slam home run every time."

What's the secret to reaching for the stars? The CEOs I spoke with said that the prerequisite for casting talent that fits the organization is to have a script: an "aligned strategy," a "corporate essence," a "common vision," or "common values." Just as in acting, if there isn't a script, how can the stars read for the part?

"The Right People in the Right Seats"

By the time executives reach senior levels, they have demonstrated skills and competence. The key to sudden impact is to make sure that your team supports your agenda and strategy. Or, if some team members have a different view, you still need to know that once the team makes a decision, the dissenters will stay on course with the group. As Peter Dolan has said, you need people who are 110% committed to your agenda.

The Left-Handed Shortstop

Dave Dorman, former chairman and CEO of AT&T, compares people selection to the fact that there are no left-handed shortstops in baseball. Why? "Because when the ball is hit to the shortstop, if you're right-handed, you can pick it and throw to first base in one smooth motion. If you're left-handed and you go to the hole and you catch the ball, you have to stop, turn your body and then throw. That creates an extra two seconds for the player running down the base line. It keeps you from making the double play.

"In a 162-game season, perhaps 60 balls that would be thrown out by a right-handed shortstop would not be thrown by a left-handed shortstop, and hence the reason there are no left-handed shortstops. It's the same reason there are no left-handed catchers. There have been some who batted left but threw right.

"In corporations, we violate that rule all the time. We take perfectly wonderful sales-oriented people and we try to make accountants out of them. We take accountants who have no personality on the phone and try to make salespeople out of them. The Bell System had actually what was called 'a fungible management practice' which is how you develop people and we were developing everybody. You rotated jobs. We made engineers salespeople. We made salespeople engineers and accountants public relations people. We just turned on the big Mixmaster and let Darwin sort out the rest."

Dorman entered his job amid the decay of the telecom industry. "My job was to say, 'We do have to rethink this and the cost structures have to be radically different.' The second piece was, 'Who do I have around me to help me do this? What skills do we have? How do we get it done? How do I know?' I had to do a crash course in the people around and whether or not they fit into the positions as I envisioned them to come."

So how do the best leaders winnow out the stars from those who just talk a good game? Are stars chosen from the inside or brought in from the outside? If from the inside, are there certain good people who are still just in the wrong job? If new stars are selected from the outside, are they people who previously worked with the leader? The examples that follow illustrate all these questions and more to explore how high-impact executives reach for their stars and what organizational contexts drive their decisions.

Ed Zander, CEO, Motorola. Ed Zander is a firm believer that you have to have the right people, and they have to be in the right jobs. Zander read Jim Collins' *Good to Great,* and says, "Whether you like the book or not, it contains one of the best lines about getting your team: 'It's the right people in the right seats on the right bus.'" In other words, the best stars cast in the right roles with the right script.

Zander concurs with other CEOs that people drive the current strategy they are talking about at Motorola, the innovative thinking and some of the cutting-edge initiatives. After 15 months, Zander sees that it all starts or stops with people. Each one is critical. The unstated paradox is that the strategy, the innovative thinking, and the cutting-edge initiatives also drive the people.

Zander started an exercise early in 2005 at Motorola based on Collins' book. He took his team through an exhaustive process of identifying the right people in the company. Then they put that aside and went through the specific top 120 seats—without putting people's names on them. Zander had each member of his team tell the group what the top jobs were in that part of the organization. Then they voted on each. Zander took a picture of the conference blackboard where they recorded all the information. He remembers the blackboard was full with a huge mural of the jobs. The most amazing thing to Zander was that they had 90–95% agreement on the results. They reviewed and voted on the top 120 seats, with 25 for the officers, which they felt were the right numbers.

Once they had the right seats and they had the right people, they went to how many of those people were in the right seats. Zander says, "It was surprising. It was one of the most difficult, remarkable things I did. I took it from that book because it wasn't important enough to just say I had the right people. It had bothered me the first year when people would come into my office and say, 'I'm the SVP of whatever.' I'd say to myself, that's a senior vice president job? That's one of the 120 seats on my bus? I'd scratch my head and go back over it."

When they separated the people from the seats, Zander says, it became even clearer. "For example, someone I'll call Avery is really great, so she's one of the 120 people. Now, the next question: Is Avery's title, VP of Communications, one of the top 120 seats? No one had thought about that question before. They just thought about the seats. You can't just give the seat up because it's one of the 120 seats."

The final part of the scenario—"the right bus"—meant articulating Motorola's strategy of seamless mobility and what the company was about. "We're still developing that. We have a bus that's moving. At this point, the bus defines whether we've got the right assets in the company." He thinks they've got some things that don't fit that, which means those assets might need to get a different bus going the other way. "One of my big objectives this year—and it's going to take a year—is we've got the bus, but we have a mismatch of right people with wrong seats. To get that all rationalized can't be done in a day. It's going to take a lot. There will be people who are de-titled perhaps. People will be moved around."

Stephanie Streeter, CEO, Banta. Having changed her team pretty quickly once she took over at Banta, Stephanie Streeter has some definite ideas about how to get the right people in the right seats. A few things worked to her advantage when it came to getting her team in place, including the fact that she'd first gained some history in the COO role at her new company, and she didn't

How to Nurture a Rising Star

To CEO Stephanie Burns, the most fascinating process in her own reach for the stars is how Dow-Corning supports its high-potential associates from around the globe. Burns thinks it is unique in the business world. The entire executive team spends half a day every four to six weeks in review sessions focused on high-potential associates—a population that is openly identified across the company. The senior team invites each of the identified individuals to spend an hour talking one-on-one with the executive team. These individuals talk about their career, what they value, what challenges they have, what successes and failures they have had, and where they want to go. Then the executive team spends time in dialogue with the individuals on their development plan—how are they going to get where they want to go. Burns says that the development plans typically get recycled two or three times.

For example, the executive team might question a class being proposed or suggest a certain experience or global location that the individual has overlooked. It is a very in-depth session. While it may sound intimidating, Burns says it isn't because individuals know up front that they are not there to be critiqued. The executive team is passionate about helping its high-potential candidates get ready to use all of their capabilities.

Burns adds, "Generally, at some point the question will get asked, 'If you were sitting in this room, what would you do differently?' They all have wonderful answers and ideas. So it's a two-way street. It's a global process so we'll have Chinese, Japanese, Europeans—everyone around the world will come in for this. Invariably, there's some mentoring that takes place afterward because some member of the senior team decides to follow up on an issue for one of them. It's all very good."

have a looming financial crisis that she had to focus on. She found that asking others in the company about who the stars were wasn't very effective: many senior members were fading stars but their followers couldn't see it. Instead, in her first five months on the job, she visited every facility and met every management team—a full 40 manufacturing facilities around the world—and asked a lot of questions of those team members in order to identify the real stars.

Streeter believes that if you ask enough questions about how people run their business, you find out how they think. She'll ask, for example: "So, how do you solve root problems? Are you the first to recognize them? When something goes wrong are you asses and elbows in trying to fix it? What's your sense of urgency? How do you motivate the people who report to you? How do you think about the future—or not? Do you use external data or not?"

According to Streeter, these kinds of questions can reveal much about how people go about solving problems. "Take an issue that you see coming on the horizon, and ask people, 'Did you notice this? Are you doing anything about it? How are you involving people? How are you involving the outside world?'" Finding stars for your team is easy once you ask those kinds of questions, she says.

For Streeter, that kind of questioning led her to conclude that she couldn't reach out for many stars inside Banta. Thirteen senior team members are new in their jobs or are new to the company in the last three years. Only two were promoted from within. Overall, Streeter decreased her senior team from 20 to 18—still larger than most other CEOs' teams.

To get the best people, she found that she had to be creative about how to work with them. For example, she has allowed a lot of her team to live away from headquarters. That puts a greater burden on her and some of the other people in terms of communication and travel, but she says it's worth it if you really have the right people.

When Streeter joined Banta, the corporation had 8,500 employees; it now has roughly 8,000. By surgically removing people, Streeter sent the message that the organization had to change

Smile at People

"I have this saying," Banta's Stephanie Streeter says. "When you walk through a factory, frown at the equipment and smile at the people. Most CEOs smile at the equipment because they paid a lot of money for it. They don't realize that every day the difference between that equipment and how it runs is in the people who operate it. I'm an introvert and it's not easy for me to interact that way, but you get so much out of it. When you need those people to walk through walls for you, that's what makes them do it, not anything else. It's the contact and the understanding and being eyeball to eyeball. You're a real person. I'm a real person. Let's do this together."

and become more efficient and effective in every role. So even though the changes in headcount may seem small, they were nevertheless perceived as huge because they had a very dramatic, quick impact. Streeter sees the effect at Banta as "evolution vs. revolution." In other words, you can get big, noticeable results even through evolutionary, small steps. *Sudden* impact in an *evolutionary* way? Streeter says the secret is you have to pick the right things—and in a smaller company, "You only need about 25 people to make a difference. You just have to find them! And they have to be in the right positions."

Dick Notebaert, CEO, Qwest. "I don't think it takes long to figure out who should be on your team, and it's usually mutual," says Dick Notebaert. The important thing is to build on both the organization's and employees' strengths, he says, and not dwell on the areas of weakness. He recalls, "The company had multiple organizations, and integration had not been completed. So we quickly moved to do that. We had over 180 executives and now we're around 80. Of those 80, many are recent additions.

"When it comes to getting people motivated and getting the right team of players in place, the most important thing we did was as a group—management, nonmanagement, and union management—was to decide that making the company survive was our ultimate goal together. Customers equal work equals jobs. That's why we reduced management before we ever touched nonmanagement. People who thought they were safe because they were in IT found out that "customers equal work equals jobs" applied to them too, and to HR and to legal. Nobody is safe. Yes, that creates anxiety—but a little anxiety is a good thing."

Stephanie Burns, CEO, Dow-Corning. Stephanie Burns has had a long history with Dow and therefore had a lot of information with which to choose the stars on her team. Before becoming CEO in July 2004, she had served as Director of Women's Health at the company during the breast implant scare of the mid-1990s, which led to her promotion to EVP and put her on the inside track for the CEO position.

The story of Burns' rise to the top is important to understanding how she chose people for her team. From the variety of her experiences, she knew that the people around her were always very important to her success and the company's. She knew them personally from working with them hands-on in all her experiences over the years, whether in the sciences, in Europe, in the breast implant crisis, or in the strategic teams she led as executive vice president that resulted in restructuring the company. Burns' entire career and her organic ascent to CEO meant that unlike CEOs parachuting into an organization, she knew who the stars were on her team and where to reach for new stars. She didn't have to guess or rely on instincts. An additional high-impact factor was that as EVP, Burns was given the opportunity to advise on appointments to the senior team made by her predecessor.

Of Burns' 12 executive team members, none were in place before Burns became EVP. "About half came into their roles when I did, and since then we've turned over six or seven positions. I was asked for advice by the then-CEO. I was very blessed because from day one he conferred with me. He said, 'You're coming into the number two position. Let's talk about the other existing positions. Here are the people, pluses and minuses.' When he changed out a person through retirement or for whatever reason, it was fully up to me to approve the successor. He said, 'You're going to be working with them a lot longer than me.' He was just really wonderful."

Finding stars outside the company isn't easy—nor desired—at Dow-Corning. Keep in mind that the company is in Midland, Michigan, in the heartland of the state, which presents somewhat of a recruiting challenge. The closest metropolitan area is Detroit—which, unless you're in the automotive industry, isn't a draw for most high-potential executives. Dow-Corning hasn't traditionally brought a lot of people in from outside the company, but Burns did bring in a few. She brought in a human resources director and a general counsel from the outside, simply because Dow-Corning hadn't grown talent that was ready for those positions. Her feeling is that if you go outside it has to be to get someone who's really head-and-shoulders above internal candidates or to specifically bring in another view or a different culture. She realizes it can be demotivating if people are aspiring to more responsibility, especially in some functions such as manufacturing where there's a track to the top job. As Burns postulates, if promotion from within always seems to be an impossibility, then you tend to lose your stars.

To attract talent and develop common values, Burns and her team spent a lot of time on the company culture. They needed an updated, clear strategic vision about where they wanted to go. Sub-sequently, one of the executives led them through a process where they took a step back and asked, "What is the essence of the company?" They didn't want to lose the "we" of Dow-Corning as they moved forward. They identified what they value, what their customers value, and what their communities value. It has become what they call their *Competitive Essence*. They believe strongly that the culture of the company differentiates them. They found that the Dow culture is one of "we want to solve problems, we are extremely friendly with a high degree of ethics and follow-through on commitments, and we are passionate about our customers."

Burns underscores that the *Competitive Essence* overrides all of Dow-Corning's direction because without it, the company isn't going to move forward successfully or have the right talent to support its growth.

Andrew Liveris, CEO, Dow Chemical. Like Stephanie Burns, Andrew Liveris also was an insider—"organically grown" in the organization—before he took the helm. Because he believes in the power of his team's collective intellect and judgment, he says, he was very deliberate about how he chose his people. Moreover, he went about selecting them in some surprising ways—like asking the other candidates for CEO to stay on in the company after Liveris himself was appointed to the job. Not standard practice in corporate America, to be sure. The story of his own succession to Dow Chemical's top job illuminates how Liveris went about picking his own stars.

Liveris, whose lilting Australian accent belies a razor-sharp intellect and latent iron will, became CEO at age 50, having been recruited by Dow straight out of college. Part of the appeal for Liveris was Dow's promise that if he joined the company, it "would show him the world." For more than twenty-five years, Dow has kept its promise to Liveris. His dream of traveling the world has been fulfilled—and then some. His three children were born in three different countries, and he lived and worked on multiple continents. Like many of Dow's senior leaders, Liveris has leadership skills grounded in extensive, hands-on global experience. (In fact, four of Dow's top eight jobs are held by international citizens, as are 40% of the top 200 jobs.)

After a leadership role as head of Asia-Pacific operations in Hong Kong, Liveris landed at headquarters in Midland, Michigan, in the late 1990s, running a large division. Then, in 2003, Liveris' entire world changed. Although Dow had always been a family-led company, the Dows had the foresight to put in place a clear succession plan when the first non–family member became CEO. The plan requires an automatic rotation when the incumbent CEO turns 60, which is young by today's Baby Boomer standards. As the incumbent approaches that age, the organization goes through a relatively automatic rotation. The outgoing CEO becomes chairman, and the inbound CEO is announced and becomes a new member of the board.

Twice in Dow's history that cycle has been disrupted—the second time in 2003 when Liveris assumed the seat. By the end of 2002, the energy crisis was escalating and the external world was falling apart after 9/11. Dow had merged with Union Carbide and the board was seeing quarter after quarter of deteriorating financial performance. The previous CEO, who was in the chairman's role, was brought back to rescue the company and appoint a successor. Upon his return, he put a rescue team in place—and Liveris was on the team.

By July of that year, the board began an extensive interviewing process. While the board considered outside candidates, they decided they had six viable candidates on the inside. Within a month, the field was narrowed to three people. The identity of the other two was then revealed to each of the remaining candidates. Liveris remembers the selection process that occurred over the next 90 days as extremely rigorous; the board members couldn't afford to do it twice. They had defined the leadership and personal characteristics that they felt were critical criteria for a Dow CEO. They wanted to make sure that they really felt comfortable—personally comfortable—with the person, so the board ran the candidates over every possible hurdle to get to their answer. Ultimately, Liveris was appointed COO in November and went through a one-year transition period under the previous CEO, Bill Stavropoulos. The goal was to allow Liveris to get his feet wet running all the operations while Stavropoulos handled the external demands.

Liveris learned of his appointment on a Sunday night. The first thing he did the next morning was to spend several hours with each of the other two contenders. He told them he wanted them to stay as part of his team, helping to shape the future of the company. After all, the three of them had been considered the top guns in the company. (Unlike General Electric's succession plan, where the other two candidates were required to leave the company, Dow had no such requirement.) Liveris told them both that if he was in their shoes, his head would be in a lot of places at that point, and that they should let him know when they were ready to talk about it.

A month later, one of the candidates told Liveris, "I'm going to be very straight with you. I've always wanted to run my own show. I don't care how big it is. I just want to go do it. I want to commit to you that I'm going to leave with dignity and I'm going to leave with full support of you and I'm going to leave early. I'm going to take the first thing I can find because I don't want to tell you I'm going to join and then six months later leave." For Liveris it was a disappointment to lose such a seasoned leader. The other candidate, however, remains as an integral part of Liveris' team.

How did Liveris get the rest of his team in place? When he was appointed COO, an office of the chief executive was formed with the top four officers of the company. Liveris immediately appointed a twin team he called the "portfolio team," consisting of key people who had never before played at the corporate level. He elevated people quickly because he felt it was time for a generational shift. He knew he himself was a generational shift and hoped he would be in place a decade or more. He needed to engage the right people to accompany him on that journey. When he became CEO, he integrated the twin teams. His goal was for the teams to create the continuity Dow had always embraced.

Liveris cascaded the selection process used to pick his own team down through the company. He and his team found it a very powerful process because it was criteria based. The criteria deemed important to each role were developed by the "collective you," as Liveris puts it: the board for the CEO, the CEO and the CEO's team for the next level, and so on. Liveris maintained that when teams have articulated all the criteria, evaluation against the criteria can occur against a very fair work product. If someone didn't get a job, the manager was able to provide a straightforward explanation of why they didn't get it. "You could actually be very clear and say, 'Look—right, wrong, or indifferent—this is what a lot of people feel about your skills against those criteria.' Maybe a lot of people don't want to hear that, but then they know what they need to work on before they get the next job or that they've already got what it takes," says Liveris.

Liveris had more to say about how to create a high-performance team. "There's a front end to the process where a lot of airing goes on. I need to know who you are, where you come from. I've worked with you or I haven't. How much skin do you really have in the game? Are you a politician—are you acting, where are you in your façade? When it comes down to the big decisions and you don't have perfect data, you have to have people in these jobs who can operate with both imperfect and perfect data. By the time it comes to you, a lot of brains have looked at it. So then you know that what it's down to is judgment. The team has to have collective judgment—the collective intellect of the corporation.

"You have to be able to work that team. The best way I, as the leader, can be on that team is not to intervene in the process. If a decision can't be made, of course, I can come in and carry it on my back. Hopefully, that's rarely required. I call it the 51% vote. I always have it. They know I have it. It's in my pocket. I'll use it, but I'd rather not. So for that you have to select people that you know can play that way. They have to be individualistic, and, of course, a lot of what you bring into that role is being a fierce competitor. Many have won on an individual basis but suddenly they're on someone else's team. The team has to run not so much on individualism or consensus but on collective, concise decision making— not analyzing your navel but really getting at things."

Liveris says he did not have the challenge of having to deal with fading stars as many other new CEOs do. From the original team of four, the former CEO and two other people have retired, leaving Liveris as the only original member. The team Liveris created now has been operating together for two years. He feels that at this point he's no longer the person directing or guiding it. The stars

Liveris reached for have gelled into a high-performance team. It has evolved from sudden impact to sustained impact.

Liveris concludes: "Understand that the one true lasting source of competitive advantage in a global economy is the talent of the people in your company. Everything valuable that a company creates comes from employees—products, services, technology, efficiency, discipline. In a word, ideas. So if you're going to be successful in the long term, you have to recruit and retain the best people and you have to challenge them, give them a lot of responsibility, and hold them accountable for performance. And you have to reward people for performance and differentiate among those who are average, those who are good, and those who are the best."

◆　◆　◆

As the stories from the CEOs in this chapter illustrate, to have sudden impact on the job, high-level executives need to reach for the stars—and sometimes very quickly. Impact is all about *getting* the right people on the team in the right positions. *Retaining* the right people means making sure that the bus is attractive (common values) and going in the right direction (common vision and strategy), so that the passengers want to stay on board.

Let's turn now to another common myth regarding high-impact executives—that they never err—and if they do, it's fatal.

4

REWIND

Myth #4: High-impact executives never make mistakes.

When John Parker became CEO of American Culinary ChefsBest, to his surprise he had to deal with a company culture that he didn't instinctively understand at first. In fact, if he could rewind one aspect of his job at his new company, it would have been to put more emphasis on culture right away, when he set up the business.

When he became CEO (by buying the company), eight employees from the old regime remained. The culture was very amorphous, and Parker says he didn't know right away what he wanted the culture to become. Parker feels the culture developed organically rather than his establishing, articulating, and then screening for the desired culture in the people he hired. "We had a culture but it took a while. It took people coming on board and developing it as we went. If I had a clearer vision on day one of what I wanted my culture to be, I would have made sure that I attracted those kinds of people, not only because of the appeal of what we did but also because of the culture. That would have made for less turnover on the front end, I think. They would have had a broader concept of what the company was all about. That's probably the one thing I would've done differently."

Like Parker, many of the CEOs I spoke with felt that there were things they definitely could have done better or at least in a different way. Some would even say they made a "mistake," especially in the early days of their tenures. Most leaders wish they had "gotten out in the field" much sooner with their teams, their customers, and in some cases, suppliers. They wish they'd trusted their gut and made the people decisions sooner. They wished they'd moved faster—on everything.

Even so, not one of the CEOs I interviewed thought of these early mistakes as fatal; rather, they chose to view them as crucial learning experiences. In this chapter, CEOs use the benefit of their 20-20 hindsight to share reflections on the best ways to have a sudden impact on the organization.

I Wish I'd Used My Time Differently

For Stephanie Burns, CEO of Dow-Corning, even now that the company has completed a couple of strong years under her tenure, she says she wishes her instincts had led her to manage her time differently in the beginning. Burns says, "You're so caught up in everything, trying to do everything, and everyone gets access. It takes time to let all of that siphon through to knowing truly what's important. And I'm still learning where it's important for me to spend the most time, where I need to delegate or not to be involved at all. That takes some time and practice to learn because you have so many things coming at you in terms of time commitments."

Her biggest challenge, she says—and where she needs to devote much of her time—centers on trying to drive growth in areas that are totally outside the company's traditional scope. "I'm finding the more we go in that direction, the less clearly I have a handle on what's the next step, how big is this opportunity—what's behind the curtain? We have a growth council that's trying to drive us into some of these new areas and there's been quite a bit of improvisation. We've been trying different things, bringing in different people to help us think more broadly about innovation—not just product technology but the whole gamut from innovation in business models to logistics to branding. It's really unusual for a specialty chemical company to think that way." All that, she says, takes time and a willingness to improvise sometimes.

Jay Amato's big regret also had to do with timing. If there was one place he wishes he could rewind the tape, it would be that he

My Big Regret

"I would've changed more people faster," says CEO Stephanie Streeter. "I've never regretted taking someone out. I've only regretted that I've done it too slowly. I don't know if people would agree with that, and I made a conscious decision to allow people to move out through evolution vs. revolution. But in retrospect, I think a revolution might have been better although with [the former CEO] still here, I don't know what clashes that might have caused."

Similarly, CEO Ed Zander had some definite regrets when it came to getting people in place. When he first arrived at Motorola, he says, he had inklings about some people because he'd heard things about them from others—and maybe he could have made some earlier initial decisions based on those inklings. "One of the things people say I didn't do fast enough is the people thing," he says. Every CEO he talked to as he prepared to take the job said the one regret they had was that they didn't move people fast enough. "They said, 'Ed, move faster.' And then you end up moving slower!" lamented Zander.

could have come to an agreement sooner about the terms of his new job at Viewpoint, so he might have become CEO and gotten to work on the company's problems sooner than he did. Here's how he explains the events around taking the helm at Viewpoint:

"In the 1990s, I was chief operating officer of Vanstar, a value-added computer systems and services company. I had started my career in a retail computer store, a job I took because of a cute girl who worked there." From that fateful beginning, Amato rose through the variously named organizations as the industry consolidated, until they merged with Vanstar. He grew the business from several hundred million in revenues to more than three billion. Amato had also managed to stay in his beloved hometown of New York through all the company consolidations—until Vanstar.

Vanstar was headquartered in northern California, which meant that Amato often found himself flying coast-to-coast to see family and hang out in his native city.

After six years, Amato was tired of the grind and missed the New York lifestyle. He had grown the company and more than likely, it would soon be acquired. It was time to fulfill a lifelong dream he had: to become a sculptor. So for five years, that's exactly what Amato did. He made large-scale sculpture in stone. His favorite work was a surrealistic sculpture of what looked like a target. It started as a 750-pound block of limestone and took about a year to finish. As Amato tells it, "There was one thing about stone that I really liked, that I thought was representative of me. It was the only art form—and clearly the only sculpted art form—where you took away from something. That was how you actually made it, instead of starting with something and building up from it. You started with it and took away from it."

Viewpoint started talking to Amato in December 2002 (he didn't end up accepting the job until August 2003). Originally they approached him to be president and clean up the organization. As he explored the opportunity, he found that the CEO didn't really want to make changes that Amato thought were important, including downsizing the role of the CEO if a president joined. If Amato were to join Viewpoint, he wanted to be able to move quickly to fix the problems. They also couldn't agree on the equity portion of his compensation. That to Amato was a signal that Viewpoint wasn't serious about change. So in early 2003 he passed on the opportunity.

In mid-2003, a friend of his on the board approached him and reopened the idea of joining Viewpoint. The board member assured Amato that the CEO was stepping out of the way. The company had still not brought in a president. Instead, they'd had consultants and operations people walking in and out the doors. By the time they came back to Amato about the CEO position, the company had burned through another $6 million in the first quarter.

Amato says today that if he'd been able to come to terms back when he first talked with Viewpoint, he might have helped stave off the damage better. In the interim, besides the $6 million of valuable capital, the company lost a number of very smart senior technology people who had become disillusioned. And by the time Amato came in, another quarter was ending and Viewpoint had lost another $6 million. As Amato laments, "Twelve million dollars was out the door. It was ridiculous. Penny-wise and pound stupid."

What I Wish I'd Known

Banta CEO Stephanie Streeter wishes that she'd known more about the company's culture: "This might be a company whose revenues when I joined were 15% from outside the United States, but you wouldn't have known that it was 15% outside the State of Wisconsin based on the lack of diversity of thought and the lack of savvy. That's something that's really hard to figure out in interviews. It wasn't until after I was on the job that I came to recognize that, wow, there's a lot of things that need to change."

Streeter also echoed something I heard from a number of the CEOs—that she wishes she'd probed more during her interviews about how the company makes decisions. For example, she says, basic decision-making processes that one would assume would be present in any business—and therefore might not be a topic for the job interview—were missing in the organization. As Streeter recalls, "Things like strategic planning just weren't done. We didn't do line-item budgets in many of the different business units. We didn't have dashboards or scorecards or key performance indicators. There were a lot of things that I associated with a Fortune 1000 company and how it's managed on a day-to-day, month-to-month basis that just weren't done. That came as a surprise to me and would have been something good to know coming in."

I Wish I Had Acted Faster

To be sure, the most often cited "rewind" wish or regret was that CEOs lamented not acting more quickly than they did in a number of areas. They erred on the side of caution, conservatism, and compassion when they should have just done what they needed to do—which actually might have been comparatively risk-free, rational, and still compassionate.

For example, once Jay Amato came on board at Viewpoint, he told me, another issue surfaced that he wished he could have dealt with in a different way—even while he knew he really couldn't. As he explains it: "We had 120 million users, and they were never really tapped. Most of them didn't even know they *had* a Viewpoint media player because it came along when they downloaded AOL Instant Messaging or did other things. If I'd had my druthers, and long term I think it would've been more effective, I would have slowly built a relationship with those 120 million customers. I probably could have yielded a much bigger, longer business out of that than basically trying to quickly offer them an upgrade in technology. There's a huge value right now in distribution, but unfortunately because I needed to get revenue as quickly as possible, we had to take a strategy that was much less polite and much more aggressive. From a short-term perspective, it was the best thing to do because it started putting numbers on the table right away and got us to profitability sooner. I always try to tell people that unfortunately we never did what we wanted to do in the first year: We did what we could do to save the company.

"It takes a long time to get to what you want to do or what you think is best for the company long term. Some people have that luxury. Unfortunately since this company had missed its numbers so many times and never met a promise it could keep, I could never go to Wall Street and say, 'Look, give me a year or two, we won't show any profits, but I'll build a good company.' No, I needed to get profitable fast. So I think in this case, we had to move quickly on certain things that, given more time, we could've done better. We also knew that we'd lost a lot of those people who said, 'No, I don't want this' and 'I don't like you guys because you're very aggressive.'"

Amato talked about a *USA Today* article that focused on CEOs of the current generation who are retiring and ex-military. The reporter also talked to Amato, who is non-military, as a counter-point to the other CEOs profiled in the article. According to Amato, "These guys were used to a very different time. From my perspective we have to make quicker decisions today than they did. They took a lot of time to do analysis. Now the information, with decent systems, is available quicker. You don't need to take a lot of time to make an educated decision. Where faster typically meant careless, now faster is just faster."

Expressing the views of many CEOs that I interviewed, Amato continued, "Faster is better because in the absence of a decision, chaos occurs. I'd rather be right 80% of the time and come back and fix the problem than sit and wait for the situation to fester further or degrade further while we're trying to come up with the right solution. I think right now everything is about getting things done, making a decision, executing on it, and acting quickly. If it works, great. If it doesn't, fix it, change it, or get rid of it. If you know there's a problem you have to fix it. The longer you wait, it costs you more money or costs you more customers, which ultimately costs you more money."

Chicken or Steak?

CEO Jamie Dimon says that when you have a lot of decisions to make—as he did when he took his new job—there are some things that should take very little time or analysis. The alternatives are going to get you to a similar result no matter which choice you make—so you should just do it. "The point is there are certain things you just need to decide," he says. "I call it the chicken or steak question—make the decision and move on."

Like Amato, Jamie Dimon did not have the luxury of time when he arrived at Bank One. Dimon admits that maybe he tried to move a little too quickly. He recalls, "I tried to do too much too fast rather than too little too slow—because it takes a long time. I say that but I couldn't have done much more. We broke things apart. Things were hard enough as it was. I couldn't recruit enough good people quickly enough. Two years later you look at stuff and you made a mistake six months ago and you think, 'Jeepers, I should've spent more time on it.' You say, 'How could I miss that?'" As Dimon concludes, the reality is there just are things you are going to miss.

Ed Zander of Motorola feels his organization isn't yet operating at the speed and level of efficiency that it could be. "Of course, I'm hard on myself," he says. "But a high-performance organization should be like a high-performance car. Motorola is like a car racing with the big guys, or a sports team playing in the big leagues. We've got a team on the floor, and it's better than it was a year ago. But we're still not operating at championship caliber. It's kind of like a six- or eight-cylinder engine. Instead of four, we're at six or eight now—but we still sputter once in while. We still get water in our carburetor. We've gone from 30 miles an hour to 50 or 60, but we're not at 80 yet."

When It's a Mistake to Move Too Fast— or Too Slowly

With the benefit of hindsight, many of the CEOs I interviewed could look back and recognize moments in their careers when, rather than moving quickly, a slow pace would have saved the day. But again, whether to go fast or slow depends on the context. And since a key attribute of effective leaders is that they always see the positive side of events, the CEOs I spoke with tended to see things as "learning experiences" rather than as mistakes—valuable experiences from which they garnered rich morsels of advice to share.

For example, Irene Rosenfeld, CEO of Frito-Lay, says that whether faster is better depends on the subject. "Generally faster is better when you're in a turnaround situation. Mine wasn't a turn-around situation per se. Yes, I had to turn around the Quaker business but it was a small piece of the overall business. The mothership was doing just fine. The issue was just how we were going to sustain and accelerate that growth. That's quite a challenge. You always want to take care of the people. You don't want to make anyone's head spin, but even as you integrate businesses in an acquisition, it's always best to tell people what you're going to do. And then within some reasonable period of time, just do it."

Rosenfeld, who became CEO at age 50 and whose corporate photo makes her look rather conservative and stately, is actually a petite dynamo who met with me on a weekend, wearing a running suit, which seems to be indicative of the gear in which her life runs. When it comes to people issues, Rosenfeld agrees that she'd like to move faster but sometimes, depending on the situation, it is better for the person leaving—and for the organization—to let time work its way to a resolution. She says that as far as any other situations she would rewind, she felt that she had really done her homework and had the company situation fairly well pegged with what the good, the bad, and the ugly were likely to be. She spent a lot of time with her boss (Steve Reinemund, chairman of Frito-Lay's parent company, PepsiCo) to make sure they were going to be able to work together. She still thinks that that was time well spent.

Rosenfeld faced one difficult people situation that needed time to reach a final resolution, much as she would have liked to have wrapped it up quickly. There was someone in the organization who had been with the company in key positions for a long time and who had expected to get the top job Rosenfeld was offered. Yet her hands were tied. She was the newcomer to the organization. As Rosenfeld says, "I don't think I personally could have done any-thing differently."

Stephanie Burns of Dow-Corning doesn't think faster is always better. She would say there is a balance between fast and slow. "You don't want a lot of bureaucracy in your decisions, so I think you want it to be very clear what the criteria are, who's making the

What I Wish I'd Known

Bristol-Myers Squibb CEO Peter Dolan wishes he had asked more pointedly in the interview about the status of the incumbent CEO and how long he would remain active in the day-to-day business. "I think it's critical that you establish what are the first 100 days of someone's role in the job. The issue usually comes up, as it did in my company, when the outgoing CEO is retiring. Everyone wants to be respectful of them and their contributions to the company, so there's a gradual transition. The problem is that the transition obscures in the organization's mind what's the clear starting point for the new leader. In my case, having gone from being president of the company, with some businesses reporting to me, to CEO reporting to the chairman who was still here, the real question became, When is the starting point of my first 100 days? I wish I'd asked that question and made sure there would be a clear delineation, because I think it helps facilitate the very important task of getting on with finding people for your team who are not only good but 110% supportive of you and your agenda."

decision, what the process is. I do think you do need to be very methodical about it. Even though a function may know the answer, sometimes you need to be able to share the data that tells the story. You need to be fast in that you need to be clear and not postpone the decisions or overanalyze, but I do think you need to do that at about 80-90% of your analysis. That last 10–15% probably doesn't gain you much more."

Burns believes slower is better when you are venturing beyond what might be considered the traditional core expertise of a company. As she states, "If you're getting into new ventures, investments, or acquisitions that are outside of your core expertise, then you'd better do your homework."

Banta's Stephanie Streeter agrees with Burns that there are times for fast—and times for slow. And faster is definitely not always better. She says she has a saying about it: *"Slow down to go faster."* She adds, "For me it's a pretty calculated speed. I know exactly where I have my foot on the accelerator. It's just how I like to operate. I also understand that for an organization, that's not always best. There are often times where I'll say to people, 'We're confused about this because we're trying to take it too fast and we're missing some of the richness in the detail. So let's slow down so we get more people in the boat, so we ultimately can row faster.'"

To Streeter there are particular cases when that is truer than others. "When you're trying to do change, going slower to go faster is often the issue. You haven't communicated the case for change. You haven't developed the data that other people might need to understand where you need to go. The vision is still a little bit fuzzy, so how do you drive people to the place you need to go? If you're just telling them north, you're not going to get to the place you

What I Wish I'd Known

Motorola CEO Ed Zander says, "I wish I'd found out more about the company culture. I was totally taken by surprise by the utter lack of cohesion and meaning around the Motorola image and brand. I knew it was bad—I just didn't know how bad it was. I found out that the word *Motorola* didn't mean anything. M-O-T-O-R-O-L-A did not mean anything to the employees. What employees knew was that they worked for CEGIS, GTSS, ISIS, or whatever—Motorola's operating companies. So Motorola didn't have just one culture to transform. It needed to transform multiple cultures into one. My biggest challenge has been getting people to think about: What is Motorola? What does it stand for? Microsoft stands for something. Intel stands for something. IBM stands for something. For a long time, Motorola had no message."

want them to go. Change is the place where it pays off the most to take the time. Anytime you're implementing an organizational change, it needs to be well thought through."

Peter Dolan of Bristol-Myers Squibb says, "The extent to which you can make decisions quickly, obviously, it facilitates people to move on with it. Protracted decisions sometimes make sense when you need to get additional information. But if you're not going to have better data three months from now, you're much better off making the decision now."

Dow Chemical's Andrew Liveris would agree with Dolan. In general he believes that too much analysis is paralysis, and that it's a mistake to take too long to make some kinds of decisions, in particular. Large organizations die because they aren't as fast as their most nimble competitors. He says that corporations need to have a decision-making mechanism that signals when you've arrived at the point where it's judgment—where all the data and analysis have been done and answering the next question doesn't add anything.

"Most decisions in our business are strategic and have to be done with long cycles in mind, so they already have gestated in the organization for somewhere between six and twelve months anyway. The worst thing you would do in a decision process like that is stalling. If you're at the point of knowing what you need to know—then go!"

Most important, Liveris says, is to gauge the speed required for making a decision based on the type of situation. For example, the time it takes to fill a position in the company depends on the role. "On the people front, there was perhaps one mistake I can think of that we've had to recover from. But really, of all the tough decisions that had to be taken about filling positions, I can't think of one that I look back on now and really regret."

Generally, the area where CEOs seemed to most wish to rewind the tape was to have moved more quickly on people issues, although some believed they couldn't have gone any faster even when speed might have been needed. As far as strategic decisions, once you've got 80% of the data, most CEOs would say: *move*—as

quickly as you can. When they talked about whether faster is better, the CEOs I interviewed seemed to agree that the context dic-
tates the speed.

◆ ◆ ◆

Contrary to popular belief, then, no matter what mistakes they
might have made—and whether or not they think of them as mistakes or learning experiences—the executives in this chapter obviously have been highly successful. Missteps do happen, but they
don't necessarily matter much if they do not significantly change
the company's outlook or if leaders make timely course corrections.
Let's look now at another common myth: that the most effective
executives have reached a point in their careers where they no
longer need mentoring or advice.

5

A LITTLE HELP
FROM MY FRIENDS

Myth #5: High-impact executives are lone rangers
who no longer need mentoring and advice.

Dick Notebaert stepped into his CEO job at Qwest thinking, "How hard can this be?" After all, he had been a CEO before, and in a company—Ameritech—with roots like Qwest's, in telecommunications. At Ameritech he had magnificently crafted the sale of the company to SBC, another telephone company. Notebaert was looking forward to being able to benefit from his experience.

But within six months of arriving at Qwest's Denver headquarters, Notebaert figured out that his experience wasn't going to be enough. As already described in an earlier chapter, Qwest was in serious default with its creditors and an entirely new set of financial covenants had to be negotiated. Having run a clean company at Ameritech, Notebaert found that this presented a new challenge. He knew he needed help, and he turned to his former CFO and his former PR guru to get him through the crisis. Had he known the magnitude of the problem up front, he could have avoided default and would have been able to obtain more favorable terms for the company.

Today, with 20-20 hindsight, Notebaert says that first off he would have brought in more help to resolve the problem—such as a whole new team of financial advisers.

It's lonely at the top. All the CEOs I interviewed mentioned at some point their surprise at just *how* lonely it can feel to be the person in charge, the one to whom everyone turns to for advice and answers—in short, the one to save the day. The pressure can be intense. Contrary to what many people might believe, however, even people at the top of the organization still find that they need outside sources of insight, camaraderie, and mentoring.

Friends in High Places

To whom do top executives turn when they need to get advice about a thorny problem, or just to let off steam? The CEOs I spoke with relied on a wide range of sources—including but not exclusively peers.

Dave Dorman, CEO, AT&T. Dave Dorman is one of the best at cultivating and maintaining friendships that he can rely on for support. Known for his laid-back style, he has traces of a Georgia drawl, a quick wit—and anything but a laid-back approach to business. Dorman, who became chairman and CEO at age 44, joined AT&T in December 2000 as president to run the core business, which was consumer long-distance services and business enterprise services and "pipes" (wholesale services).[1] Before Dorman took the helm, the previous CEO had decided to restructure because of a significant debt load that, given the market conditions at the time, the company couldn't get refinanced. Of AT&T's $65 billion in debt, more than half was short-term debt that historically hadn't been a big deal because AT&T's cash flows were solid. The company had always been able to borrow and pay back short-term debt very easily. But with the changing market, that advantage slipped away quickly.

Moreover, when the restructuring decision was made, no one at the company could have guessed that the tech sector would melt down or that fraud would be revealed in a number of telecommunications companies. As Dorman says, "We were simply looking at our business and saying, 'We don't know where all this ends but we believe that the industry is in for a very rough ride.'" The business model had to be "sliced and diced" so the company could work its way out of a structure that had produced the $65 billion debt load. The restructuring included the IPO of AT&T Wireless and the acquisition of AT&T Cable by Comcast in an unprecedented $72 billion deal.

"The Comcast intervention helped us in our de-leveraging objective, but with wireless already gone, it forever strategically changed the options that we could have in play for bundling," says Dorman. "That was the environment in which I became CEO. My first challenge was to pick up the pieces, create a new future for AT&T, and get the balance sheet further pared down. By the time I became CEO, we'd reduced debt from a peak of $65 billion—our net debt was about $56—to a net of $5 billion, which was a reduction of $51 billion."

Further, after Dorman's promotion to CEO, the pricing of AT&T's product lines declined a real 70% in one of its businesses (Dorman defies anyone to find another business that has had 65% of its revenue experience a 70% price decline over a five-year period). The rest of the product line suffered major price declines as well. "We had this completely unstable pricing environment driven by a supply and demand imbalance and recapitalization. We couldn't crawl out of it. We couldn't say that by 2005 everything will be peachy keen. My job was to say, 'We have to rethink this. The cost structures have to become radically different.'

"The second challenge was: Who do I have around me to help me do this? What skills do we have? How do we get it done? I had to immerse myself, doing a crash course in the people around me, most of whom I inherited from the previous CEO. I had to figure out whether or not they fit into the positions as I envisioned them to come."

With these two tasks looming, Dorman certainly needed help—advice and insight. Fortunately, if anyone had learned how to develop networks of friends, it was Dorman. But rather than looking solely to peers for help, he relied on members of his new team and his old teams, as well as former mentors, outside advisers, and board members.

There were a couple of people Dorman relied on immediately. One was Chuck Noski, now the former CFO, who—like

Dorman—had come to AT&T late in the game. Noski was up to his eyeballs in the balance sheet restructuring. Often after everyone else had left for the day, Noski and Dorman would get together in the office and carry their conversation into dinner. They'd talk about where they were and what they were trying to get done.

Surprisingly, Dorman also went to the longest-tenured guy in the company. Who says you can't learn new tricks from old dogs? Frank Ianna, who ran the AT&T network operations and whom Dorman referred to as the father of AT&T, was someone Dorman says he leaned on a lot. In fact, if you drove up the road to AT&T's headquarters, you'd realize how much Dorman admired Ianna. Upon Ianna's retirement, Dorman named the main drive into his offices Frank Ianna Way. Dorman characterized Ianna as a "thirty-year guy who bled AT&T blue and was passionate about the business." Ianna had seen a lot of people come and go. He was as smooth a politician as anyone would expect for a vice president at AT&T, but he genuinely cared about the company and the people and he was very respectful. Says Dorman: "Frank didn't get to where he was without understanding when you have a boss, you are obligated to tell him what you think. He always did his best, with a maturity and commitment that really came through."

Dorman, unique among the CEOs I interviewed, also used outside consultants to help him assess who should be on his team. "I decided it was an impossible task for a CEO to get inside a 20-year career and say gee, I can really get to know this person. It's not like when you work side by side with someone for a long period of time. So I used coping strategies, one of which was to use a psychological firm. An industrial psychologist came in to do a three- or four-hour interview with people and assess them, so I could get objective information. I needed to be able to say, OK, here are this person's strengths, weaknesses, and personality—and how does that stack up?"

Dorman also points to his outside legal counsel as someone who provided help and advice. "He's a very wise, very unflappable guy who has persevered through many difficult situations," he says. "He was a very calming influence when I really needed that."

He also conferred with Bill Esrey and Ron LeMay, both former CEOs of Sprint (where Dorman had spent the bulk of his career). Today Dorman primarily relies on his board of directors for advice, insight, and camaraderie, especially the six of them who really lived through the company crisis with him.

Dorman went on to make a point that many CEOs I interviewed shared, that his head of HR is also one of his most trusted advisers and more of a one-on-one coach. "Mirian [Graddick-Weir] will tell you what she thinks—and what she thinks is right on."

At the end of the first quarter of the year he was appointed CEO, Dorman brought in people who had been on his teams previously. His general counsel and HR head were the only ones who stayed on but a lot of people around them in the legal and HR departments have changed. The rest of his direct reports are people he brought in. He had the advantage of having been in the industry for his entire career and with the downturn in the telecom industry, he knew key people who were looking for jobs—some of whom have become close advisers as well.

Dorman also relies on what he calls his "kitchen cabinet" (a term used by many U.S. presidents—including Ronald Reagan and dating back to Andrew Jackson—to refer to their closest advisers, whom they trusted to give them straight answers). Dorman's kitchen cabinet includes Tom Horton, John Polumbo, and Bill Hannigan—his two operating heads and his CFO, respectively.

Stephanie Burns, CEO, Dow-Corning. Upon taking the helm at her company, Stephanie Burns says, she turned to a lot of people for advice, including some in high places, such as Andrew Liveris of Dow Chemical. Given the size of Midland, Michigan, they may be the only two CEOs of Fortune 1000–sized companies in town and of course, the companies are related, which gives Liveris special insight into the kinds of issues Burns faces. Burns also had a couple of colleagues who are CEOs in the industry. She feels very confident about the advice they give so she says she doesn't hesitate to phone them and say, "Hey, are you doing business in China? Are you experiencing this and that?"

Burns says she's never felt "lonely at the top" because, having grown organically into her job at Dow Corning, she knows the people and they know her. She gets a lot of feedback across the organization. She says, "I don't feel disengaged, maybe because I'm relatively new in the job. I feel like I can go out and talk to anybody. People show up in my office. We're a very open culture. You don't even have to make an appointment. You can just come in and say, 'Hey, I was just thinking about this' or 'Did you know about this?' Maybe over time, you get a little more disengaged because of your work activity and you don't interact at all levels, but today I don't feel lonely at all."

Andrew Liveris, CEO, Dow Chemical. Initially upon becoming CEO, Andrew Liveris didn't have a "kitchen cabinet" to advise him. Since he had come to his position from within the company, as CEO he found himself suddenly leading all the people who had been his peers. One person he turned to for advice and support, therefore, was Bill Stavropoulos his former boss and the acting CEO when Liveris was appointed. But he also sought out other CEOs who were best in class. He identified who he wanted to talk to and through mutual contacts, lined up in-person or telephone time to learn their secrets. He wanted to understand how they entered their position and what they learned that he could take back to his new role at Dow.

As Liveris tells it, "I said to myself, OK, you're going to be compared with others. You don't know what that looks like. You read books, you talk to consultants, but you haven't played. You should go talk to people who have played. I asked Bill Stavropoulos if he minded if I did that, and whether he had some relationships out there that he could endorse. I just e-mailed or picked up the phone and said, 'You're a great CEO. . . .' I went to a selection of the 500 successful companies—the ones that you'd imagine. That was one group. There were maybe a dozen in that category. Then I did something else. I went to customer CEOs. These were big companies too. I had two objectives there, of course, especially when I was appointed. I said to the CEOs, 'Look, I'm the new guy at Dow and I want to hear everything you want to tell me about how you see Dow. What could be better? What can we do? At the same time I want to learn about you and how you do your job.'"

Liveris certainly caught his customer CEOs' attention. They weren't used to being asked about their jobs. It was a great way to develop camaraderie that is valuable both as peers in the business world and in their personal career experiences. Liveris took extensive notes and has implemented some of the things advised—such as putting all the vital company initiatives on a one-page "scorecard" that outlines the organization's goals and its progress toward them.

Liveris also sought out additional advisers. Starting from his early days in the company, Liveris had mentored about 35 people at Dow, and now that he's CEO he has found that he can count on those same people to tell him when things are really wrong. He knows their concerns are legitimate because they have no agenda. Over time, he has also found other members of his team who are strong and comfortable enough in their own roles that he can bounce ideas off of them in a really productive way as well.

Other Sources of Insight and Advice

Colleagues and other folks inside and outside the organization aren't the only sources of help available for the CEOs I interviewed. Several heads of smaller companies, such as John Parker, mentioned organizations such as YPO and WPO (the Young Presidents' Organization and its alumni group, the World Presidents' Organization), for example, as an extremely helpful source of advice and counsel.

When Even a Top CEO Can't Help You

How would you like to be friends with one of the most influential CEOs in the world and be able to count him as a member of your "kitchen cabinet"—only to realize that his advice, through no fault of his own, hits far from the mark when it comes to your company's situation? Such was the case for Jay Amato.

Amato counts Steve Ballmer, CEO of Microsoft, among his close friends and advisers. About a year after his appointment as CEO of Viewpoint, Amato went to see Ballmer. Here's how he describes it: "He was talking about Microsoft. It was right around the time that they announced their big dividend. I asked him about the circumstances of the dividend and he started going through all the reasons why they were giving it. Then he said to me, jokingly of course, 'Plus it's kind of fun to be able to screw with the Gross National Product.' [Because the dividend made such a bump to the GNP.]

"I felt like saying—'Come on, I'm struggling here!' I wasn't even trying to grow Viewpoint. Viewpoint is a small company so the best case we had was to become more of a 'thought leader.' It would take us a long time to be a leader in a market. So there I was talking about having $800,000 worth of revenue on a mature product—and he's talking about the GNP!"

John Parker, CEO, American Culinary ChefsBest. Parker has been a member of YPO (and now WPO) for twenty years and says that the organization has really felt like his own personal board of advisers. The average YPO chapter has eight to ten meetings a year consisting of dinner and a speech, says Parker, plus monthly meetings with your "forum," a small select group that you meet with to discuss business issues. Parker says 80% of the issues are the same across businesses: things like personnel, sexual harassment, accounting, and strategy. What is said in the forum stays in the room, and it's only for members, vs. the chapter meeting where spouses are invited to attend.

Before he bought American Culinary ChefsBest, Parker had owned radio stations in 11 states around the country for 20 years. "I never had a board. YPO was my board. My forum group was my board. I couldn't get a better board than the forum because you had twelve company CEOs of like mind and experiences. As a budding CEO, I found that the people in the forum had a tremendous reservoir of experience and they were totally objective. They didn't have a vested interest. They'd shoot it to you straight. You could bring up any situation you wanted and the group would discuss it and bring out the relevant issues."

Parker went on to explain the concept behind WPO, the organization you move into from YPO once you turn 50. "The idea is that by the mid-century mark, your mind-set changes. You've built your company, and now it's a more mature entity. How do you bring life into a mature company? And you start to think more personally. What's your *personal* plan? What are your goals? You're going through the midlife issues: how do you handle those? Personally, I think now most people start considering these questions when they're closer to 60, but the point is that you're in a completely different place from the YPO, forty-ish mind-set."

Pat Russo, CEO, Lucent Technologies. For Russo, some of the best advisers have been her board members. Her former CEO and chairman, along with the lead director on her board, are people she talked with frequently, especially in the first months on the job. The former CEO has played a very important advisory role. Certainly, he has lived the challenges with her, preceding her on the wild ride through the telecom market. Russo says he's always there for the company and it's been really important. "It's great to have a sounding board."

Russo says she has a couple of "kitchen cabinets" but they involve members of her team rather than outsiders. She elaborates: "I would say the cabinet I rely on most includes the CFO and probably the general counsel. We get together and talk about issues sometimes. It used to include the guy who runs business strategy and development occasionally. I try to engage my whole senior team in a lot of the things we do and decide because I want people invested in not only the policy but also in the organizational strategy. A lot of the policy and things we do affect the organization and the people." She's come to the point where she doesn't "do much kitchen cabinet" although the demands of the business environment require her to spend a lot of time with her CFO.

Irene Rosenfeld, CEO, Frito-Lay. Rosenfeld says she consciously selects her team largely for their ability to function as advisers. Like other CEOs, she often turns to her (new) head of HR and finds her chief legal counsel can often be a terrific asset. Rosenfeld also includes her chief strategist as very helpful. She says, "These are typically the folks who can step back a little bit with more objectivity and stay above the politics. I spend a great deal of time with my CFO, my sales and marketing folks, but at the end of the day, the people who are not in the fray are in the best position to step back and so I use them most often as my sounding board."

Moreover, while she also relies on a number of her friends outside the company, she has found they just don't have enough information to be helpful in certain situations. When it comes to specific contexts where she needs objectivity, Rosenfeld has turned to an organizational consultant. "They don't know all the players, so they're able to give advice based on solely their instincts and business expertise." For example, during the time she was coming on board at Frito-Lay, Rosenfeld went through an invaluable "new leader assimilation" engagement with an outside consultant who has done a lot of work with the parent company, PepsiCo, over the years.

Stephanie Streeter, CEO, Banta. Streeter says she is close with her whole team, and depending on the subject matter, sometimes turns to specific individuals for advice. Probably as a function of parachuting into the company, Streeter admits, she finds it lonely at the top "because you make all the decisions, and there isn't anybody who has the same perspective within the company that you do. But I learned a long time ago that I'm not smart enough to do all of these jobs. I really do run the company as a team and while I'm the final decision maker, I involve a lot of people. I am constantly getting different perspectives."

Streeter says she also relied on several outside consultants and coaches whom she has grown to trust over the years. For instance, one external consultant specializes in organizational development, and she asks him lots of questions. She occasionally calls on a woman who has been her personal coach since her stint at Avery-Dennison. Streeter also talks to her spouse a lot. Not only is he wise, she says, but because he knows her so well his advice is tailor-made for her. It helps that he is a former businessperson. She says he has a lot of insight into her; sometimes in her rush to the finish line, he'll be able to slow her down a little bit. She reflects, "I'm not the kind of person who will go in a room, close the door and just figure it out. I think that helps, but I have a tough job. It is a real grind." Talking it out, she says, can really help.

Jeffrey Joerres, CEO, Manpower. Joerres believes that if you can build a relationship with your organization, you can get all the answers you need. As he says, "Your people have to feel unafraid to talk to you, even though they're always going to respect your leadership position. Of course, you'll get people who hate you for whatever reason. You're going to get that in an organization of 27,000 people, but if you get the majority of them really respecting that you are trying to do something, you are trying to listen, then you really have a great asset. This isn't your HR person taking you by the ear and making you do roundtables once a month or that kind of thing. They know I'm genuinely interested. And I've come back from talks with people with the most incredible knowledge that has saved us a ton of time and money.

"I believe that my role in this job is defined by what I don't do, not defined by what I do. On any given day, I'm asked to approve a project, to go down this path or that path. All you hear about are the things we decided to do, but what really defines my role, and in essence the company's, is what we decide not to do. For example, I've decided not to do certain things because a staffing specialist making $20,000 a year said, 'That's stupid.' After I heard it from five or six different people, it resonated with me too that we were going down a path for the wrong reason. So I went back to my senior team and said, 'Guys, we need to rethink this.' My team says, 'Well, where are you getting your information?' I say, 'I talked to Jim, I talked to Joe, I talked to Susan, I talked to Nancy—not as scientific as all your PowerPoints. But guys, it makes sense to me.'"

Community boards have also been a prime source of wisdom for Joerres, especially in his earliest days on the job. At those board meetings—for example, a civic committee focused on regional economic development or the board of his alma mater, Marquette University—he could witness firsthand several very good CEOs wrestling with an issue. "You didn't just see how one person operates, but rather there were three, four, or five at one time. I actually could start to see how they were thinking and analyzing a problem."

Peter Dolan, CEO, Bristol-Myers Squibb. Dolan agrees that it's lonely at the top, but that he also has a number of people in the company that can advise him on certain issues and who clearly play the role of kitchen cabinet. He also worked with an organizational change consultant who was instrumental in helping him design the leadership forums that Dolan organizes. Who else does Dolan turn to for insight on particularly thorny issues? Like Streeter, he talks to his spouse. "She has been an indispensable source of advice and support."

Dolan has also found it important to call on friends for support in other ways—outside the business context. For example, he has a very personal commitment to breast cancer research and finding a cure, not just because of his company's interest in oncology, but also because his family has a history with the disease. As a result he's become very involved in organizations such as the American Cancer Society and the C-Change of Cancer—a group consisting of both for-profit and nonprofit companies. As an initial personal effort to contribute to research, Dolan, an avid biker, undertook a cross-country ride for fundraising a number of years ago. Ever the competitor, he was determined to do more. What better friend to reach out to for a cause than Lance Armstrong, whom he'd gotten to know through fundraising for cancer research groups?

"This will be the tenth year that I've done a two-day, 200-mile bike ride to raise funds for Dana Farber. Lance contributes one of his yellow jerseys that I auction off for contributions. This year I'm very close to generating $1 million in contributions from people who personally sponsor me in this. Lance's jersey last year auctioned off for $138,000. That was a good start." And that's what you could call relying on good friends.

◆ ◆ ◆

As this chapter makes clear, contrary to the "lone ranger" image many CEOs project, even executives at the highest levels and with the most relevant job experience still need and do seek advice, insight, and mentoring, and they find friends in many places. Still, most CEOs I spoke with rely primarily on people inside their companies—people who see the challenges on a daily basis and are most capable of being knowledgeable, empathetic sounding boards and advisers.

Next I turn to Myth #6, regarding the pace of an organization—and explore the question: Is faster always better?

6

THEY'VE GOT RHYTHM

Myth #6: High-impact executives always quicken
the pace of the organization for the best results.

Since the day Stephanie Burns stepped in as CEO at Dow-Corning, she has found that the company's particular rhythm isn't always speedy. It's completely customer-driven—and that's not something Burns has wanted to interfere with. "The organization's pace is fast or slow, depending on what's happening with customers. You probably wouldn't spend more than ten minutes with someone from Dow-Corning that they are not talking about a customer, an application, or a new opportunity," she says. "Most of the people at Dow-Corning love to solve complex problems. It's kind of like, 'Give me something that hasn't been solved and let me have at it,' whether it's a customer issue or a manufacturing process issue. They thrive on that challenge. They work well in teams. I don't think there's a team in Dow-Corning that doesn't cross multiple functions and multiple geographies."

Not surprisingly, in the past five years, she says, the company's rhythm has become much more globally oriented and aligned with a much clearer vision of where the organization is headed.

The point here is that—unlike what many people might assume—when it comes to achieving results, moving faster or even making an organization's overall rhythm smooth and melodious does not always equal "better." Like good drummers, executives create the best organizational music when they can vary the pace here and there, or (as Burns does) allow the company's own customers to help determine it. Sometimes success means encouraging and acknowledging some dissonance. Sometimes it means pausing the action, creating some space in the intervals between major events.

Many of the CEOs I spoke with, like Burns and like Jay Amato, whose story follows, didn't think that they necessarily had to jump into an organization and immediately quicken its pace in order to achieve the best results (although some did—and we will look at those as well later in the chapter). For new leaders to be effective, they must sense the rhythm of the organization and whether changing the rhythm will result in greater impact—or not.

Slow or Fast—It's the Pause That Refreshes

When Jay Amato took over at Viewpoint, he walked into a company that needed to play a major game of catch-up if it hoped to succeed. You would think, then, that Amato would have immediately tried to jump-start the organization, making some fast decisions and getting products moving out the door one on top of the other. But he didn't. As discussed earlier in this book, Amato moved quickly to rid the organization of a lot of executive overhead in order to conserve cash. Once he accomplished that, he strove first for a kind of harmony inside the company, an environment in which the remaining people could accomplish what needed to be done, working together in a measured and nonpolitical way. That doesn't mean that people don't disagree, Amato says. But he thinks that the reason the company has been able to accomplish so much is that before taking action, there is first a lot of discussion about what people on his team and elsewhere in the company want to do.

Once a decision is made at Viewpoint, however, everyone runs fast and hard—together—to get it done on time. When I interviewed Amato, the company was in the middle of one of these periods. A new version of their product was about to be released. Amato characterized it as a "psychotic time" for the company. "Everyone's working super late hours," he said. "When I instant message someone, I see people still at their desks at ten, eleven o'clock at night or one o'clock in the morning." He stresses that part of the momentum is due to people respecting a decision, moving with it, and not continually challenging it once the collective has decided.

But then the following month, he says, after the goal has been met, the company will go into a quiet period, and its pace will become almost dormant. "We'll take a few months to see how things are going with the product, pick up the pieces, and clean up from the damage we did when we were running so hard for those few months to get these products shipped." Soon after, the company enters yet another phase, when it begins asking, What's the next step? "We'll ask, 'Is the plan that we decided on still good? Do we need to change it?' And then we go for another all-out run." Rather than a constant fast and furious push forward, then, Viewpoint goes through various rhythms of slow thinking through, high-speed acting and implementing, then resting again.

Joerres' "Rapid Incrementalism"

When Jeffrey Joerres first became CEO of Manpower, he remembers that the big question on people's minds whenever someone took over a company was, "What's the transformation strategy?" But Joerres has never been a big believer in such strategy, which to him sounds like "you blow the place up and start over." Instead, the right thing for Manpower when he came on board was a rhythm of "big spurts, then quiet time," though he says that today the rhythm of the company overall has become more even.

Rather than "transformation strategy," then, Joerres advocates a concept he calls "rapid incrementalism." He says there's value in making sure you know the steps required to get to the destination— perhaps phasing in a strategy rather than blowing everything up and starting over. "When you're a visionary only, you look through binoculars and you can see a long way and you can see where the Promised Land is. But when you take down the binoculars, you say 'Holy smokes! There are seven rivers and two mountain ranges in between. I didn't see those in my lenses.' That's why I said that our organization had to get much better at rapid incrementalism. You've got to run like hell, but you can always stop and adjust. The strategy has to be built on solid platforms. If you do that, once you are through with an initiative and it gets its life and behavior in the organization, you can get on to another initiative."

Rapid incrementalism, then, is this ability to take on major initiatives, for example an e-commerce initiative or a branding strategy, but, as Joerres warns, "You can only do so many of those. If the organization is doing things incrementally, you aren't afraid to make mistakes because you don't have big mistakes. Big mistakes come from big transformation proclamations: We are going to do this in 18 months. Then we get there and say this isn't right either. That's when you see CEOs rip out the management team and start over." Joerres makes sure that his people understand that it's OK to make mistakes, "because we're going to make mistakes in a way that we can recover from them. So don't be afraid. Get out there and start running."

Joerres says his approach has created an energy in the organization that was absent previously. The view now is "we can keep running faster and faster and get this whole rapid incrementalism right, which means no one can catch us because we're too slippery." People are changing a lot in incremental ways all the time all over the business. That, Joerres asserts, is the difference he has created in the organization's pace.

As for his own personal rhythm, Joerres says he strives for balance. He really loves working but he doesn't like working for things that aren't going to lead somewhere. He sees a lot of potential for that in the CEO job. "You can really be busy and have a lot going on, but to me that is insulting to the organization because the organization is going to say 'enough of this yin-yang.' When I look at my role in the company, I think it is about the intensity of initiative and focus, with the ability to say: 'You know what? We're not going to take ourselves too seriously. We're going to have some fun doing this. I'm not going to be right all the time. No one is, but this is where we're trying to go.' People respond to this straightforward approach. And getting that kind of buy-in is where I get most of my satisfaction."

Part of Joerres' personal rhythm includes frequently picking up the phone to talk to people in the branch offices. He thinks it's the best way to find out how quickly or slowly head-office initiatives are cascading through the organization. "It's amazing how honest they'll be. More often than not, the feedback is we're on track. But sometimes they'll say, 'I didn't even know you guys were trying to do that.'" Joerres loves going back after a few such calls to his executive management team, which thinks all the processes are working fine. Joerres will say, "I just talked to two people, guys, and they don't know what the hell we're doing."

That kind of interface is precisely what Joerres sees as the primary role of a CEO: to build constructive alliances out in the field. That's why he fosters functional alliances where people can be honest with each other without fear of retribution. He's not looking for one right answer when he calls or stops in a branch office. "I visited Paris and walked right into a branch and said, 'I'm here. We're trying to do this. What do you think about this? What do you think we should do about that?' If they can sense my personality, though they've never met me before, then I can get dialogue from them that I can do something with. Sure, I could instead simply send out documents or give presentations about what's happening. But that isn't enough. We need direct interaction."

While Joerres says that periodic interactions by phone or in person determine a lot of his and the organization's pace, he says too that for him, rhythm is about knowing when to act or not. "There is this cadence to a company and as a CEO, you can feel the cadence, not be told what the cadence is, but feel what it really is and it makes the job easier. You slide in the right initiative at the right time and it creates more momentum, and then you slide in the next one. You can slide in an initiative and maybe it slips a gear slightly, but you have enough momentum to keep it going."

Russo's "Rhythm of the Numbers"

For Lucent's Pat Russo, the question of rhythm rang a bell. "My CFO is always talking about 'the rhythm of the numbers.' We're always asking ourselves, 'Do we like this rhythm or not?' The rhythm of the organization has been and continues to be: get better, get better, get better. It's a constant gotta do more, gotta be more efficient, gotta find more growth. We just keep pushing and slugging it out, trying to learn from mistakes. I think that's positive, but it's also hard because nothing is easy in this industry anymore, even though there's still lots of opportunity."

On the other hand, Russo says, that rhythm of constantly pushing forward sometimes, by necessity, gets interrupted. For example, when Lucent goes through periods of resizing, Russo says, "people keep looking for an ending to it, keep hoping it's over. They want to believe it's over because we've stabilized, we're growing, and we've had our seventh quarter of profitability. But what I say to people is the nature of our business and our industry requires us to be simultaneously downsizing in some areas and growing in others. That's the nature of what it is we're managing through and we have to have a simultaneity about our capacity to lead and manage and think that accepts that as the reality we are operating in."

For example, the downsizing has come at the same time as a Lucent initiative Russo called "developing great talent." "Some people question how you can develop talent when at the same time we're reducing headcount in some of the mature parts of the business. My answer is we have to. We can't stop the investments in the things that are going to help this business grow while we are managing down the mature parts of our business that, to accomplish anything, require good, cogent business decisions. It's heartbreaking. It's very hard for people who are being affected by that. It's hard to do. So that kind of thing definitely interrupts the rhythm. It's disruptive to have a reduction in the organization."

But there are more positive ways that the organization's rhythm can get interrupted, she says, for example a big win like the Cingular UMTS contract. "It's a big deal for us. We said we must win it, and we did. So there was this period of constancy and then there was a quickening of the pace in reaction to the positive effects of the deal."

Regarding her personal rhythm, Russo suspects it is probably more forward-looking than the organization's. As she puts it, it's her job to always be asking, "What do we need to be doing?" And then, "It's a strategically oriented rhythm, the rhythm of a leader. That means I can't be simply mirroring the organization. Rather, I have to monitor the organization and my team to see they are making appropriate progress, where are the gaps, how do they shore them up and what else they might need to do."

Dorman's "Outside-in" Approach

Similarly, Dave Dorman of AT&T felt that his personal rhythm didn't necessarily mimic the organization's—nor that it should. Although he told me he thought that the company was moving at a fairly steady pace, Dorman said he himself goes "all over the place. I'll go like hell for four days and just immerse myself in something. Then I'll pop up, breathe deeply, and collapse for a day to think." He's a night owl who generally sleeps only five hours a night and always has his BlackBerry with him. He labels himself a 7x24 person when it comes to business, rarely going an hour without getting back to people, even as late as 1 A.M. Since he finds it so difficult to separate business from his personal life or weekends from weekdays, he works seven days. He says he'll do intense periods of two or three hours and then step back and think. Often he'll go out for lunch and talk to someone he hasn't seen for a while. He intersperses his intensity with "outside-in." He tries to look at things through other people's eyes. He's an outside-in person, not an inside-out person, while his two operations heads are inside-out people—complementary rhythms to his.

Although AT&T's rhythm as an organization has become smoother during his tenure, when Dorman first arrived as president he walked into a company that had gone five quarters without a clue. "If it was said we're going to do X, they'd do Y. Way off." AT&T wasn't used to experiencing such big misses. Up until that time, the company had been utterly predictable, no surprises. In terms of rhythm, it had been even-paced. No syncopation, no staccato. It just didn't miss. Then all of a sudden, it was totally inept at forecasting—similar to what happened at Lucent with the telecom market. There was a lot of denial; people kept thinking it couldn't fall any further. As Dorman says, "They went into completely uncharted water. It was ragtime. The inputs went crazy and everyone wanted to know what happened to the predictable rhythm of the organization. People didn't know which end was up, especially as they were doing financial forecasts, where they faced the new rhythm head-on." Dorman realized that AT&T was a company that craved predictability, so getting the organization more even-paced became a top priority when he came to the job.

Dolan's Dealings with "Crisis Rhythm"

As for Peter Dolan, who took over as CEO of Bristol-Myers Squibb in May 2001, within six or seven months his team was fighting one fire after another: "crisis rhythm." Dolan and his team were literally dealing with whatever was popping up and how to solve it as quickly as they could while keeping people focused on the company and its strategy: moving ahead and the future.

Dolan was at somewhat of a loss to describe his personal tempo during that period. Dolan's predecessor was still there as chairman of the company. He was going to leave toward the end of 2001. Dolan was new in the role. The rhythm was about somehow trying to fashion out how to work together in anticipation of when the chairman left the company, drawing a line in the sand as to where Dolan was clearly in charge.

By the end of 2003, things settled down at the company, and the organization's rhythm slowed and steadied a bit, as if the company was catching its breath. Dolan kept everyone focused on the horizon while doing the hard work of delineating what the company's strategy would be, given the hard realities they faced. Then, in 2004 and 2005, the company was able to begin building on successes and further embedding the strategy.

Today, Dolan thinks, the company's rhythm is even and steady, everyone confident about what the R&D organization has delivered. It's launched four drugs in the last two and a half years, which is very good by industry standards. It is anticipating two releases and more that are on file right now with the FDA. Dolan attributes the change in rhythm to the fact that the company moved from being very dependent on accessing outside technology for future revenue to being more driven by the fruits of its internal R&D effort. That is a big change for the company over such a short period. It affected the company because people had to believe in R&D to make the challenges and trade-offs in their business units to fund further investments in R&D at a time when there were question marks about how much R&D had delivered in the past.

When Faster *Is* Better

Thus far this chapter has primarily covered CEOs who either kept their new organizations at a steady pace or else even slowed it down a bit to assess the situation. Let's hear now from other top executives who took the opposite approach in their new positions.

Jamie Dimon recalls the rhythm of Bank One soon after he first came aboard in the Chicago offices. "I called it combustion," he says. "At some point we all moved up to the same floor, and suddenly you could see all the senior people together, you could see stuff going on and meetings taking place. You could actually feel the hum." He said that while the new space in New York has a strange floor plan, a similar hum has begun to happen as the new team has melded.

When he first started at Bank One, Dimon would go away for a week on a global business trip, and he felt he had to call in to make sure the momentum continued in his absence. His team used to make fun of him for it. They would shout from office to office. "It's Jamie on the line." He'd be transferred on the phone down the line of offices in the Chicago headquarters and Dimon would say, "Hi, how're you doing?" Dimon says today the company is running to its own rhythm. They don't need his kind of attention. He doesn't need to ignite the combustion anymore.

What is Dimon's own rhythm? He says he is a rock band—fast and loud. "When I was in Texas, people told me to slow down so they could understand me!"

Stephanie Streeter has worked to change the rhythm of Banta since her arrival at the company. "Plodding" is the word that comes to Streeter's mind to describe Banta's rhythm prior to her joining. She elaborates, "Plodding and symphonic because there was definitely a conductor at the top. There were sections. The winds were over here, the horns were over here, the percussion was over there. Now I would say we have a much quicker tempo. We're not quite rock and roll, but we're getting there. So the rhythm has picked up, it's much more following a beat and getting more extemporaneous but with a framework around it. The rhythm ebbs and flows a little bit, which is fine."

What's Streeter's personal rhythm? "Mach 4 all the time. I love change. It's my job to create—not chaos—but to always be questioning things, to create a cadence and a beat that makes everybody else pick up theirs. It's not being busy for busy's sake. Boredom is my version of hell."

Motorola's Ed Zander considers his own rhythm to be pretty fast. Don't forget he's a New Yorker. He can't stand PowerPoint slides. Zander is a "let's just get it done, tell me what you got to do, net it out" kind of leader. He says it's just the way he learned how to do things in his very first job. He knows he has to have more patience at Motorola than he has in other jobs because of the nature of the business and the complexity of the current organizational structure. But his instinct is to try to speed things up.

Zander started out in computers in the 1970s. It was survival of the fittest, very competitively focused. After being at Motorola for months, he didn't hear anyone talk about competitors. In his earlier career, he remembers they would live, eat, and die their competition. To this day, Zander begins the day with the *Wall Street Journal* to see who's announced what and what's happening in the market. He wants to know Nokia's org chart better than Nokia knows its own org chart. He wants to know its cost structure.

To Zander, his rhythm includes a sense of unbelievable customer competitive focus, speed, execution, sense of urgency and time, punctuated by the overall quality in the decision-making process and in all they do. As he used to say about some managers at Motorola (who are no longer there): "You know there are a couple of ways to ski down the mountain. I'm the kind of guy that tries to get down fast. I'm a really ugly skier. Then there are the other guys who have the great form. We both get to the bottom.

"I think you have to have some type of cadence to what you're doing, especially a company of this size. The team has to have a stake in the ground around a process. I think in certain areas of the company you need a cadence. You need a playbook. You need to have what GE calls 'the operating system.' We called it something different at Sun. Each of them addresses the organizational issues. How are we going to do leadership development? How are we going to do strategy? How are we going to get our numbers? How do we measure ourselves?"

Zander's goal is to not have meetings. For him, it's all about output and deliverables. You're going to propose a new diversity program for the company to Zander? It better be outcome-based, not lots of "chatter." For example, he heard an announcement that someone at Motorola was holding a meeting on diversity. They were putting together a *plan* on diversity. He throws out those kinds of announcements and yet people hold such meetings in companies all the time. Zander tells it: "You hear them say, 'Oh, I'm going to have a meeting. I'm going to get people together so we can do our goals, do a plan. We're going to go do a customer survey.' BS to that. Tell me how you are going to improve customer satisfaction or achieve better diversity. Get to the point. Having said that, the best companies are the ones that can do audibles in the huddle. I don't think we're there yet because they're not used to me yet, and I don't think we as a team are ready to call audibles."

Dick Notebaert describes the rhythm of Qwest as "hectic" when he first arrived. Although today the organization has struck a comfortable, confident pace, in his first days and months, he says, everything was focused on the short term. It had to be, given the financial reality of the company at the time.

"There's a great story," Notebaert says. "An employee sent me a note saying he couldn't get something done. I immediately got it done for him. Then the supervisor e-mailed me and said, 'Dick, you've got to stop this because I hadn't gotten that employee an answer yet, and then he e-mails you and he's got it.' My response back to that manager was: 'You should've done it in less than 24 hours. It's not that hard. Get your priorities right.'"

Irene Rosenfeld, when asked about the rhythm of her company, said: "What is the fastest speed? What comes after allegro? In fact, that's what I love about Frito-Lay. But it is a train moving so quickly that sometimes it moves before it knows what its destination should be."

Rosenfeld says her personal rhythm mirrors the company's: "Allegro, multi, multi! I am a quick study, both mentally and physically. I have a very high energy level. Most people who know me will say that about me. They're always running to catch up. Because of that, and I know that about myself, I try to remember to ask for feedback: Am I going too fast? Was I not clear? Should I have handled that differently? That helps me understand how the organization is receiving my message and my style."

Andrew Liveris of Dow Chemical says that his personal tempo, like Rosenfeld's, is "high energy—as fast as you can get. Sometimes I find I have to temper that with my team, but they're pretty close to my tempo now." Rather than his mirroring the organization's tempo, Liveris believes, the organization has quickened to match his own.

When it comes to Dow's rhythm, he says, "We are the ultimate network company. We invented network before network became fashionable. We had our own term for it. It was called a matrix— it's been written up in business school studies. Even so, Dow doesn't operate by organization charts. Dow operates almost like a dot.com—through personal relationships, networking, and knowing how you can leverage knowledge from one part of the company to another. Maybe it's the company's family roots that create a lot of the noise. I would say that Dow Chemical is like a Jamaican jungle drum—very noisy and dissonant with multiple rhythms. But ultimately, the rhythms all come together with a similar beat and tempo and sound beautiful. They create a lot of noise yet are integrated.

"So not only are we networked, we are integrated, meaning not just physical integration at the factory level but also people integration. We leverage work processes very effectively. We are very productive as a result but we have a central repository of knowledge that gets leveraged throughout the company. We call them expertise centers or technology centers, focused on everything from IT to human resources to manufacturing work processes and so on. Dow then runs as one company. We are 43,000 people strong and $44 billion strong. We have people in 159 countries and assets in 79 countries. You can imagine trying to run the pulse of something that is so interconnected, so complex in a way that it creates a lot of friction points."

Liveris continued with the analogy of Jamaican jungle drums. "A Jamaican drum band has multiple rhythms, and on their own the drums don't sound like much. Together they sound great. I think Dow's rhythm is like that. The flip side is that we worry here at Dow when things go quiet. I worry when I don't hear anything."

John Parker describes American Culinary ChefsBest's rhythm as fast-paced and very adaptive. Parker says, "It's organic from the standpoint of continually adapting on a daily basis, as any species should if it wants to survive. That is kind of our rhythm."

When Parker bought the company, he was essentially moving it over to a whole new business model. "I did it so quickly that I really didn't worry about the past because I knew where I was going," he says. "As we're building a new industry, so to speak, and a new business in the industry and developing a process that is new, we have to continually be very sensitive to everything around us to make sure that we stay on course and that every day we are doing things the best possible way we can. It's that proverbial airplane that is off course 99% of the time, as all airplanes are, but they're always correcting and that's why they always get to the airport they're going to. The rhythm here is to be like that—to be so sensitive that we're always adapting and we're always getting as much information as possible from all aspects: our judging process, our internal systems, our industry, and what is needed by our customers. Every day we adjust like an airplane does on a flight."

◆ ◆ ◆

One of the most intriguing things I found when interviewing CEOs was that these leaders were keenly aware that their organizations had a rhythm, and they were respectful of that fact. They also recognized that the organization's rhythm often was not the same as their own personal rhythm. What's more, they knew that in order to make change happen, they needed to understand when to go with the rhythm and when to interrupt it to be most effective. Fast was not always good nor was slow always bad. And as is the case with most of the myths examined throughout this book, the truth of it really depends on the context. As important as sensing the pace or the beat, even the hardest-charging CEOs agreed that organizations require pauses to sustain effectiveness. The intervals in-between are as important as the pace.

In the next chapter we consider intervals in the context of organizational change, and look at the myths surrounding how soon a new executive can be expected to produce tangible results.

7

NET 90?

Myth #7: High-impact executives need to make a
major mark on their companies by the end of their
first 90 days.

In January 2002, not long after Peter Dolan became CEO, Bristol-
Myers Squibb spiraled into crisis. While pharmaceutical companies
are quite regularly the target of lawsuits, Dolan came into his job
with an inordinate number of legal challenges to defend. Far from
being able to make a mark or achieve results within some preconceived time frame, Dolan spent his entire first year and a half as
CEO simply trying to fight fires.

Finally, toward the end of 2003 things settled down a bit, so
that by 2004 and 2005 the company began building on its success.
When I interviewed Dolan more than four years into his tenure, he
told me that, when it comes to making an impact on a company, he
didn't believe in destination points.

"I'm better at this job today than I was four years ago, partly
because I always viewed my whole career as a journey, not a destination," Dolan said. "I keep looking ahead for new experiences and
reflecting back on experiences, and I keep learning from them."

The first question on many people's minds when an executive
steps into a new position is: What will get accomplished in the first
90 days? Certainly this is true at the CEO level, where shareholders
and industry analysts eagerly await the new leader's initial quarter's
company results. But as Dolan's story illustrates, despite that implicit
expectation of the CEOs I interviewed—all successful by any measure—they didn't necessarily make a tangibly measurable impact
within the first 90 days. In some cases it reflected a conscious decision on their part to just lie low for a while and assess the situation.
In other cases, like Dolan's, they had little choice in the matter.

But whether they made an initial sudden impact or not, the thing that all the CEOs I spoke with mentioned was how quickly (or not) after they entered their jobs they began to feel they'd attained a kind of equilibrium, or flow, in the company. Call it what you will—"in the groove," "all cylinders firing," "hitting your stride"—reaching that place was what these CEOs felt was key to making a real impact on the company. Sometimes that happened quickly—but more often it took a little time.

Let's look now at a few other CEOs who, like Peter Dolan, discovered that finding that place of flow wasn't necessarily a quick or easy process.

Steady as She Goes

Jeffrey Joerres of Manpower says that in the early months and even the first year or two of his new job, rather than trying to make an overtly big initial impact, he was more interested in listening to what was going on within the company, grabbing the nuggets and piecing them together. It was about being enterprising more than intellectual. More than anything else, "I had to become a bit of an alchemist and pull all this stuff together," he says. "Even now that I'm in the groove, as I enter my seventh year as CEO, I think I still need to do that. It's what gets us from here to there. The speed has gotten faster, which has been by design because we've sped up the pace of the organization. So as the pace quickens, you have to be able to do this alchemy much faster. But I feel that once you're in the job for four or five years, the world changes on you—in a good sense. In an organization this big, it takes three to four years to get real behavior change. Now we're starting to see where it worked, where isn't it working, what's catching on and what's not."

Joerres was willing to wait it out to see the results. He believes that timing is everything and that, as a leader, you have to sense when your team is ready. All this, he says, is why he does not like the idea of a short tenure in a top executive position. It doesn't demonstrate the capacity of the leader and it takes organizations

The True Role of the Leader

"I've heard lots of definitions of leadership," says CEO Peter Dolan, "and one that I think is particularly apt is to think about the role of the leader as creating, conserving, and channeling energy. Creating energy is energizing people, getting them charged up. A leader can have a big impact on raising the amount of energy by celebrating successes, building up momentum, and getting people excited about where the company is going. Channeling energy is about alignment, which most people would say is one form of leadership. Conserving energy is basically recognizing that energy is a precious commodity. You have an ability to influence it, to some extent, by creating energy and channeling it—but people ought to be thinking about energy from an organization as having a somewhat finite capacity. The degree to which you can transfer the organization's energy to your objectives is a function of your ability to create and simultaneously conserve energy.

"For the organization, conserving energy is about consciously eliminating the things that bug people every day, administrative burdens that nobody seems to care about. It frees up organizational energy and allows you to channel it toward more productive uses. From a personal standpoint, I think that it is very apt as well because I think that, certainly in a leadership role like this one, you need to manage your own energy, and you need to do things that allow you to personally create energy and conserve it. What I would've said three years ago is creating energy for me is exercising. It's always been important to me. I work out three to five times a week. I have for 20 years. People ask how I find the time to do it and the answer is it is an energy-creation item for me.

"Today I would say I also get energized by interacting with people on a personal, high-connect basis and seeing the lightbulbs going on for them, in terms of what we're trying to accomplish and where we were going. Conserving energy is figuring out a way to compartmentalize the difficult and challenging parts of what you do, because you could work 24/7 in this job and ultimately that's not a winning hand. You need to consciously think about taking days like Friday off—which I try to do—as a conscious way to conserve personal energy."

some time to effect change with someone new at the helm. He says he couldn't imagine if he blew it and 18 months after he became CEO, another CEO came in and that person blew it and then another came in, because there is an internal struggle CEOs have. "There is this feeling that you want to have made a marked difference on the organization. But that CEO churn and desire to make a mark forces too much change every two years when a new CEO comes in because someone didn't produce quickly enough. . . . It's knee-jerk. By definition, it almost has to be, especially in a big public company. A guy gets fired and you hire me. Are you actually going to say you think your predecessor was right? You can't do that. You have to change it all."

For Joerres, it took a full two and a half to three years to effect significant change. "We had a lot of fixing to do. We had a recession. It was a double whammy. It took that long—and I came from the inside—which is why succession is so important. If you can develop from the inside, you've won 90% of the battle."

Despite all this, Joerres still was able to point to what he considered some early wins—although they might not have been easily identifiable to outsiders. From early on, codifying the values of company was his main preoccupation. "It sounds so basic, but the previous leaders of the company hadn't done it." To do this, Joerres brought people inside of the company together to talk about what Manpower stands for and why they thought Manpower was better than its competitors. When he asked people what the company's values were, they all said something different. Yet Joerres could see that while they said things differently, at the root they were saying the same thing.

Joerres says Manpower was always a values-based company but the values hadn't been articulated universally. He decided at the outset of his CEO tenure that this was one of the most meaningful initiatives he could start. So he put a team together that would spell out Manpower's values.

He recalls everybody saying, "We know what the values are in what we do, but we have to show the world what we can do. We need to come up with what are those values, across borders and across segments of the business."

Even this initiative didn't happen right away, and certainly not within the first 90 days. It took about 18 months to roll out the company's statement of values. Joerres was thrilled with the result. He says, "It came back as a really big feeling of success for me, because we had about 20,000 people in 60 countries—and they were all saying, 'This is what we're about.' It gave me permission to say, 'We're doing this one way now, guys. Trust us that we're going to do this right.' All of this was clearly about making people feel better about the culture and injecting some passion into what we were doing and what we stood for."

Today, Joerres' steady approach and emphasis on values seems to be paying off. "We just celebrated our 40th anniversary in Argentina and our 40th anniversary in Germany," Joerres says. "These were all-company events. I love how proud they were and they wanted to talk to me about what they see going on in their businesses. I had the time of my life."

Bank One's Jamie Dimon says there never was a time in his new job when he *wasn't* in the groove. "I was working 90 hours a week, seven days a week, and I was always making sure it got done." Like Joerres, Dimon believes interactions with people—employees, customers, teammates—are key to getting in the groove in any new position. Celebrations are an especially good venue, he says. Dimon admits he's not good at "people schmoozing" or complimenting, but he loves a good party and hanging out with people in a setting where you can really get to know them. He generally likes town halls and a leadership style of walking around and talking to people.

Dimon also admits he likes meetings. Sometimes they are boring and some stuff is just hard work, like all the systems conversions he's had to learn about on the fly, out of necessity. But Dimon feels he and the company are now in a real kind of flow after three years. "Sometimes I walk into a meeting and say, 'Do you even need me any more?' And often they'll say no. And I'll say, 'That's great!' Sometimes I have very little to do because everything's humming now."

Andrew Liveris of Dow Chemical said that while having some idea of what you hope to achieve and how you'll achieve it is probably a good exercise, "It changed the minute I walked through the door. I learned to lead in the face of change. We had to make the tough decisions, and the main thing was to stay focused on maintaining a process of fairness. We went through 80% turnover in the top 80 jobs and 35% turnover in the top 20. That is a lot of change to absorb at the top of the organization and ultimately it made a difference in how that change filtered down through the company." Liveris says he therefore felt that he did need to achieve some particular goals by about 100 days into his tenure, especially around getting his team in place. "We were in this period of relative instability, and my greatest challenge was to bring stability as fast as I could by painting the future," he says.

Liveris says that he needs to have a mind-set around implementation and execution all the time. "We manage a month at a time—with a ten-year horizon. I get daily sales reports. I got briefings last night on how we're tracking on our daily sales and daily expenses with a view to the quarter—this quarter and next quarter. It just doesn't happen overnight. You have to work it and that work is not very glamorous. You're not rubbing shoulders with the president on macroeconomic issues all the time. It's not the glamour that many people perceive."

I Knew I'd Hit My Stride When . . .

At what point do top executives know when they've finally come into their own in their new positions? How do they know that they're in the groove with their company and customers? The time frame varied. Some CEOs felt they had really found their place in the company from day one on the job. Others said it took about six months, others closer to three years—and one said he'll never fully be there.

Echoing the words of many CEOs, Lucent's Pat Russo knew she'd come to a good place in her new company when she felt fully engaged, all the time, in all aspects of Lucent. "I'm engaged with customers, I'm engaged with our sales team. I'm engaged at all levels of our business," she says. "People talk about management by walking around? I'm about management by *being* around. I'm on the phone. I'm out with people. I'm walking around. I ask people, 'What's going on?' I call the salespeople and ask them to tell me what's up. I call the head of a certain product business and ask, 'How are things going?' I'm just constantly reaching into the organization."

AT&T's Dave Dorman says that after all the initial challenges the company weathered when he first came aboard, he knew he'd hit a groove when he finally was able to stop fire-fighting and really begin to dream about the future. "Where is this all going? What will the telecom industry look like in five years and what will define a winner?" Those are the kinds of questions he's always asking himself and his staff. His industry is in a fascinating period now. "Cable wants voice. Telcos want cable. You have this cataclysmic clash finally happening. I think it's facilitated by IT networking sitting on top of the cable infrastructure for voice as well as data delivery. You can sit here and say that the Telcos are going to own X share in N years and X could be 10% to 70% and N could be three to ten years, so the constraining box is really big and trying to build a linear programming model on this, you have a lot of outcomes. So execution is really important." Dorman says the big wild card is wireless—and don't get him started talking about VoIP (Voice over Internet Protocol). His enthusiasm is contagious, and all this talk of the future is clearly what keeps him in the groove in his job.

Stephanie Burns of Dow Corning was not ready to say she was firing on all cylinders by the 90-day mark—even as an insider who had been with her company for more than 20 years. She recalls that she really felt in the groove and making an impact after about six months. The company had turned the corner financially and was, in fact, really performing well. The strategies they had put in place through all that strategic work when she was EVP and the priorities they'd set were robust. More important, the strategies were really moving down into the organization. "Everyone was saying finally we're really seeing where we're going. It's clear to us." It was at that point into the CEO job that she could say OK, now it's really about implementing this and executing it, as opposed to re-questioning it and rethinking it. That change from thinking to action signaled the direction was clear.

Dow Chemical's Andrew Liveris says, "It's not until about a year into a job that I'm able to say, 'I'm in the flow. I feel easy.' It's when things come together: my team is functioning and the organization is aligned and performing well. I know I'm in flow personally when I make more time for things I care about, like exercise and going to a basketball game and other things that I like to do. During the first 12 to 15 months in this job, I've had to really cut back on personal stuff in order to do what I've had to do.

"I think it'd be very hard to continue the intense phase of the first year or two for five to ten years. I don't think anyone should do that. If you are doing that, then you haven't set up your team and you haven't set up your organization from a delegation or alignment point of view to carry the considerable load that big organizations demand. I am exceptionally draconian in making sure that I have time to think. I normally build that time in at home at night. That's when I spend a lot of time on strategy and organization. So once I find I have more time for that kind of thinking during the day, then I'll know I'm really in the flow."

Liveris added: "People tell me I'm a hard personality. I'm driven, I'm very high energy, and I put a lot of pressure on people. At the same time, I'm fairly relaxed and down-to-earth in the way that I can be. I'm approachable. I'm as at ease with the people in the factory as I am in a board meeting. I think I learned that in Asia, actually. Being in Asia taught me how to be more calm and patient—and to live more in the moment. Lots of us fret about the future. We overplan it. But life is not like that. I mean, what aspect of life did you precisely plan years ago that you actually did in the end?"

Banta's Stephanie Streeter is the kind of person who "lives for business," and she believes she was in the groove at her company from her first day on the job. What really makes her feel in the flow on her job? Streeter responds, "Pretty much everything. I really love it when I am talking to somebody about how to make their business better—like, 'We see the future as this,' or 'We're doing it this way and we need to change this person. We need some more information over here. . . .' Business is fun—it really is! I love walking on the plant floor and talking to people who are doing all kinds of things—talking to them about what's your life today, what don't you like, what do you think needs to be changed?"

A Break in the Groove

What brings executives up short? What kinds of things potentially interrupt the flow for them, even after they've hit a decent stride in their new positions? For Stephanie Streeter, it's when she finds herself in negotiations. "I hate negotiations. I'm not a deal person. I don't like the stuff that goes on, the positioning and all that. I'd rather spend my time on the analysis and then making the acquisition work. Once we've figured out what the terms are, let's go get things done."

For Dave Dorman, it's when something happens that's utterly out of his control. "Shit happens. The FCC votes five to nothing to end one of your businesses. This gets your attention. Or it's something a competitor does. It's something that's done and you have to react to it. That's what tends to break my flow and stop me from doing what I want to do."

Dave Vander Zanden can find himself out of the groove if someone drops the ball. "We opened a new distribution center, and the team didn't follow through on everything. When we were doing the planning for it, they made it clear that they knew what to do and didn't want the executive team's involvement. Sometimes you have to let them fail to learn. When it was clear there was a problem, those associates went crazy and worked incredibly hard to fix it. Everyone now is more humble and asks a lot more questions up front on a project. It's very hard for me to let go when you can prevent a mistake from happening."

Andrew Liveris says that what would really interrupt the flow for him is if someone from his team abruptly quit and he didn't understand why. But other things could do it as well. "If there were an ethics and compliance issue that really hit at the heart of what Dow is, that would interrupt everything. By being in so many countries around the world, Dow Chemical is known for its ethics—but we're not immune to problems. I don't stay up at night worrying about this but that would definitely be the kind of thing that would come as a complete shock."

Motorola's Ed Zander said that not breaking his groove means making sure he concentrates on what's really important—and not try to be all things to all people. "Most human beings need structure. We need to have our four things to do for success. If you mow your lawn, here's the three things you need to go do, if you want to be good at golf, here are the four things. Consultants of course all try to sell us their two-by-two matrix or the five things we all must do.

"I was caddying for Trevino one day at a charity event," Zander continued. "I'm a lousy golfer, and I asked him what I could do to improve. He says, 'Do you read those golf magazines?' 'Oh yeah,' I said. He says, 'Stop. You amateurs—you're reading these things every month and they give you 42 lessons and they've never seen you play.' And he was right. We're all different. Trevino's swing is completely unorthodox. He's got a back problem. You really need a teacher who can accommodate your physical capabilities and your type of swing."

Zander says that golf lesson translates well to keeping your stride in a new job. "You really have to consider your own level of experience. You need to be very self-aware, know what you're good at and know what you need to learn and work on. Then put together a plan that will emphasize those areas."

◆ ◆ ◆

When it comes to getting in the groove of the job and achieving results, then, there seems to be no hard-and-fast 90-day requirement to get there—and most CEOs I spoke to for this chapter scoffed at the idea. As even the most savvy CEO admits, an executive coming into a new job cannot control the variables such as market conditions, financial health of the firm, or organizational readiness. Although some CEOs did feel in the groove from the start, it is foolhardy to believe that every new executive can magically be firing on all cylinders from the first day, and make a solid impact within 90 days. As we've learned from the stories throughout the book, each strategy for success depended on the circumstances in which these executives found themselves.

Next, the concluding chapter brings together everything that we've explored so far in this book—helping you look at the possibilities for managing your own first days and months in a new position.

8

THE REAL SCOOP

It comes back to really knowing where your
company is—the facts and the truth—which we've
learned may not always be discernible at the onset.
You have to assess—and have the capability to
assess—where you and your new company or
position really are right at this moment in time.
Many of the "myths" I believed as I climbed the
corporate ladder are, as I suspected (and others
have confirmed), obsolete or only one part of the
reality.

—*Dave Dorman, CEO, AT&T*

Myths pervade Western culture—false beliefs about what one
"always does" or "must do" to just fit in and to succeed. Nowhere is
this more true than in business cultures, especially as one reaches
the top executive levels of the organization. But I hope the "expert
testimony" in this book has shown through the stories illustrating
the very human side of leadership challenges, it's the *context* in and
around an organization that determines what an executive actually
needs to do in a new position.

Now let's review the real truths vs. the myths as you've learned
about them throughout this book. Understanding that the realities—and the preconceived notions that we all have entering any
new job—cannot necessarily be generalized into must-do steps will
be your best tool for formulating your own path to maximum
impact on the new job. You must listen to and understand the organization you are joining to learn what the reality is.

Myth #1:

High-impact executives encounter no surprises when stepping into their new position.

Reality #1:

High-impact executives absolutely anticipate that they will encounter the unexpected—and thrive on the possibilities.

Even CEOs with the best-honed instincts encounter surprises in their first days and months on the job. In the face of circumstances that did not meet their pre-job expectations, savvy executives immerse themselves in the issues and devise options for a speedy recovery.

◆　◆　◆

Myth #2:

High-impact executives walk into the job with a solid game plan.

Reality #2:

High-impact executives formulate a general direction for action based on the interview process, keep an open mind about the possibilities, and do as much fact-finding as possible during their early days on the job.

As we've seen, it's important to have a flexible road map. New executives need to be ready for detours, shortcuts, and complete changes in the itinerary!

◆　◆　◆

Myth #3:
High-impact executives play it safe and get to know their new teams before making changes.

Reality #3:
High-impact executives rarely have the luxury of playing it safe and are adept at weighing the risk of whether—and when— to retain or recruit team members.

In the executive suite, low-risk decisions are always better when made faster. Executives assert that the opportunity for early wins was in changing the culture or vision of the organization, not the external financial expectations, which naturally followed. Rather than changing out the entire team, more often than not, changing out a few strategic positions on the leadership team was very effective.

◆ ◆ ◆

Myth #4:
High-impact executives never make mistakes.

Reality #4:
High-impact executives know that setbacks and challenges are part of the topography of the executive office and see their mistakes as learning experiences.

Embrace hindsight. As opposed to being able to anticipate the unexpected and do the right thing, with 20-20 hindsight, executives can acknowledge that they would do things differently. In the face of circumstances or results that did not meet their pre-job expectations, savvy executives have the fortitude to devise options for a speedy recovery.

◆ ◆ ◆

Myth #5:

High-impact executives are lone rangers who no longer need mentoring and advice.

Reality #5:

High-impact executives pursue all the best sources, whether upward, downward, inside, or out, for insights, camaraderie, and mentoring.

Even the Lone Ranger needed a Tonto. Executives usually found that outspoken associates, peers in other companies, their team within the company, and "rising stars" were the best barometers for organizational insights.

◆ ◆ ◆

Myth #6:

High-impact executives always quicken the pace of the organization for the best results.

Reality #6:

High-impact executives sense the rhythm of the organization and increase the tempo only when the organization is capable of learning the new cadence.

High-impact executives invariably can describe the rhythm of their organizations. They know that the key to high impact is to understand when the organization is ready, when to interject a new rhythm, a new tempo, or a new melody that brings the organization to a new level of success. It's not always faster at the start—and, as the race car drivers at the Indianapolis 500 have learned, you need to start out following the pace car and positioning yourself as you get ready to accelerate your machine into high performance.

◆ ◆ ◆

Myth #7:
High-impact executives need to make a major mark on their companies by the end of their first 90 days.

Reality #7:
High-impact executives don't fall into the trap of putting a time limit on success. They make their mark by maximizing results for the organization on a time line that fits the organization's unique situation.

High-impact executives have a tentative game plan for success but keep an open mind and do as much fact-finding as possible during their early days on the job. They are not rushed into decisions or attempts to make their mark based on a calendar; instead, they base their work on the needs of the organization and its stakeholders.

All of the CEOs I spoke with when preparing this book agreed that, to be operating at the executive level, you must already have a proven track record of achievement and know how to play the game—the expectations, the rules, the rhythm, the team. But most important, you need to understand that the playing field and the rules are different in every organization and in every step up the ladder. Any top executive—no matter how high up in a company—essentially needs to be willing to start all over again.

◆ ◆ ◆

May the realities I have shared in this book get you onto the playing field as quickly and as effectively as possible—while helping you to understand the new rules and realities for maximizing your impact on the job.

A FEW FINAL WORDS

"My Best Advice"

I asked the CEOs that I interviewed for this book: "If you could distill all of the wisdom you gained from starting a new job at the highest level into just three key pieces of advice, what would you say?" Some of their answers focused on people issues, while others focused on the business itself. Sometimes what one CEO said directly contradicted the experience and advice of another. But always the answers were illuminating and offered a small window, at least, onto the thinking of some of today's most successful, high-impact leaders.

What follows are just some of the nuggets of wisdom that the CEOs I spoke with wished to share with anyone stepping into a new executive job.

CEO Jay Amato

1. Think fast—make decisions right away.
2. Listen to the people at the doer level—that's where there's a lot of honest insight.
3. Always keep in mind that just because it was tried once, that doesn't mean it won't work.

CEO Stephanie Burns

1. Don't lose track for a moment of who you are. Don't lose track of your values and what's important to you. Early on you are bombarded with so many opportunities. The first month or so is just a blur. You're with the media. You're with employees.

You're with your executive team. You have to always go back to your family values, your personal values, and the essence of the company. Build on those three dimensions but don't lose them.

2. Don't think you have to do it by yourself. Your executive team is always more powerful than you are in terms of creativity and helping with complex issues.

3. Do something about the fact that your business operates in a global market. Right now we're even questioning, as a senior team, why a lot of us are sitting in Midland, Michigan, and why we're not spending more of our time in Asia.

CEO Jamie Dimon

1. Don't promise anything other than that you will do your best. Don't give anyone a forecast, don't say that's the end of the management changes. Don't say I'm not going to sell that division. Just don't do it. You'll get a lot of pressure to make promises but you'll get yourself backed up against the wall. Don't do it. When I spoke with the analysts the first time, I had no new policies, no forecasts. I said, I'll tell you what I think I know, when I know it. But I always reserve the right to change my mind. Always.

2. Make sure you have some good people with you. That's not so simple. You have a lot of people who are saying, 'What do you mean, why did you pick them—why not me?' These are the very same crummy people that got us there in the first place. It's a terrible situation. The bullshitters will bullshit you too and all of a sudden you are where you were before.

3. Take time to get to know everybody, but then have a real game plan. At some point you should stop just running and get something that says, "OK, here is my diagnosis of the patient. We've got this, this, and this." And then just tell the people.

CEO *Peter Dolan*

1. Focus 100% internally. When you become a CEO, you're suddenly operating in a different atmosphere with lots of opportunities both within the industry and more broadly participating in various platforms. Some of these are necessities, like being in the industry associations. Some of them are fun and very interesting to do. But they all take time. You'll have ample opportunity later to take advantage of external things. So for the first two years, stay 100% focused on running the company.

2. Get the right people in place as soon as possible. Not only must they be competent, they must be committed 110% to your agenda.

3. Manage your own personal energy. Whatever helps you do that, figure it out.

CEO *Jeffrey Joerres*

1. Write down a list of what you are trying to do. Really write it down. Don't write down some bullets. Don't say, "I thought about it." This should be hard to do. If it is easy, it is probably being trivialized. If you're asking your guys to help you, you're probably doing it wrong.

2. Absorb the culture that the company has—really get into it. If you've been with the company in the past, it's easier to do. If you're new, it's too easy to skip across the surface of the company's culture and not think it means anything. If you don't get the culture, you'll never get the cadence. The culture may be bad, but you'd better know that; otherwise you never get the cadence right.

3. Do not make broad proclamations. There is no need for it. It may be therapeutic for you but it isn't for the organization, and it will come back to hurt you. You feel like a big shot when you do that. "And we will be the first, largest, biggest

blah, blah, blah. . . ." It feels so good! But you can say the same thing without the proclamation power. Instead call on people's passion. Ask them, "Don't we need to do this? Don't you all need to help us get there?" That's a whole lot different than saying, "I proclaim. We will . . ." When you do that, it's going to come back to you like a boomerang.

CEO Dick Notebaert

1. Be yourself. Remember where you came from—and that you are still learning. You don't know it all.

2. Don't take yourself too seriously. Enjoy the perks and all the pomp and circumstance—but don't take any of that too seriously.

3. "Touch the learner." That's a phrase I used to hear in college. In other words, see the world through the eyes of others—the customer and your employees. Put yourself in the other person's shoes before you come out with a negative reaction. That's especially true when it comes to customers. It's all about relationships, and the only way to create relationships is to see the world through others' eyes.

CEO Pat Russo

1. Spend some period of time just listening. If you're a CEO, people tend to hang on your every word. So, especially if you're new to the company, spend some time listening, ask questions, talk to people throughout the organization, form your own judgments.

2. Unless the company's in crisis, don't do anything for the first 30 to 60 days you're there. Just get a lay of the land, get a feel for the culture, get a feel for the people. Ask everybody if they were you what are the first ten things that they'd get their thoughts around. You'll get some really interesting responses.

3. Seek out other CEOs for advice and support. Ed Zander came and talked to me for a couple of hours. It was in his first 30

days, I think. He said, "Tell me what it was like. You just went through this a couple of years ago. What did you do?" You need to be able to commiserate with someone. It's a lonely job.

CEO *Stephanie Streeter*

1. Be yourself. I see a lot of people who say, oh, I love the results that person got. I'm going to try and be like Mike. But there's only one Mike. When the chips are down, you're not going to be able to be somebody else, and you know what? The chips do get down. So be yourself.

2. Trust your gut. There are so many times the information says one thing and your insides are just screaming at you: *No! No! No!* So trust your instincts. The decisions I've made that I've regretted have been because I didn't trust them.

3. Make the people decisions faster rather than slower. If you think they're right, they're right. Sometimes the only way to change people is to change people.

CEO *Dave Vander Zanden*

1. Hire the best people you can find.

2. Get rid of your ego—you are going to be wrong more often than you think.

3. Create a culture based upon mutual trust and respect.

Notes

Introduction

1. *Newsweek*, September 12, 2005.
2. Korn Ferry Survey, 2004.
3. Accenture Survey, 2004.
4. During my travels around the country to interview these new leaders, I was amazed to find that most of them, even the celebrity CEOs who received lots of early press, were genuine and down-to-earth in sharing their stories. Many showed up for the interview alone, without an entourage. And unlike my traditional image of the pinstripe suit in the corner office, most were in shirtsleeves, many in shirts sporting their company's logo. One CEO was wearing blue jeans. Even Jamie Dimon—from a banking tradition of pinstripes—was wearing a long-sleeved blue shirt with the JP Morgan Chase logo. Clearly, the tie industry is not thriving by the CEO crowd's patronage.

Chapter 1

1. Bank One was since bought by JP Morgan Chase, and Dimon was recently named CEO of the combined organization.

Chapter 2

1. Amato left Viewpoint at the end of his two-year contract to

start a new venture in the entertainment industry, Anonymous
Pictures.

Chapter 5

1. Dorman has since retired from AT&T.

Acknowledgments

This book first became a concept when I left the arms of Mother Bell in 1989. Since then, many other arms of encouragement have been extended to me along the way.

First are my two daughters—Kate and Jen—who were always patient as Mom blazed new trails, and dear friends Rita Daugherty, Katharine Boyda, Katie Chambers, Beth Summers, Rachel Fiske, Bob Russell, the Dream Queens, and the Wednesday afternoon salon who never doubted (out loud anyway!) that my seemingly unattainable dreams would become reality.

To the many people I have worked with over the years who have been inspiring as true leaders or teachers: Dennis Carr, Denny Strigl, Dan Latham, John Johnson, Carl Grivner, Betsy Plank, Nancy Albertini, Tom Touton, and Bliss Brown. To those who supported my own leadership along the way, especially Martie, Nancy, Judy, Phil, Mary, Vicky, Mary Jo, Billie, Sandra, Cheryl, Therese, KP, Larry, HB, Maggie, and many others too numerous to mention. A very special thanks to Cohort 5, Ram, Peter, Terese, Jim, and the visiting faculty from Benedictine University's Ph.D. program, who helped me crystallize my thoughts and findings into the seeds of theory. I am grateful for the patience and wisdom of my editors, Byron Schneider and Lucy McAuley, as well as the many associates at Jossey-Bass who have supported this effort.

Ultimately, this book could not have been written without the generous candor and cooperation of each of the CEOs in the book. I am humbled by their generosity. I also need to thank those folks who were my "one degree of separation" in helping me to get to the

CEOs: Kathleen Finato, Joanna Riopelle, Roxanne Jackson, Dave Vergo, Barbara Beck, Patti Hart, Beth Zacher, Karen Dillon, and Bob Puissant. As well, there were many PR people and executive assistants who are the wind beneath their leaders' wings and were a great source of assistance to me.

One last note, thanks to the many unnamed persons I have met along the way who offered encouragement to me in countless ways to stay on the path. A special thanks to Avery and Elliott—for their inspiration as leaders for the next generation.

About the Author

Susan Quandt is the retired president of the consumer sales division of 21st Century Telecom Group (now RCN). She has over twenty years of industry experience in marketing, business planning, strategy development, innovative marketplace approaches, and management of start-up organizations.

Quandt's innovative marketing skills are based on consumer goods marketing practices, applied to high technology. She developed these marketing skills and instincts with S.C. Johnson Wax early in her career as a market research analyst on major brands. She began her career in telecommunications with an AT&T operating company, where she was part of a business research think tank conducting some of the earliest research in cellular technology and developing the first flat-rate long-distance pricing plan in the country. She later joined the business sales organization, where she developed a financial selling-skills training program for account executives that was subsequently adopted nationwide by AT&T. At divestiture, she joined AT&T Information Systems, was part of the team that started up the Midwest Region, and was later appointed sales manager.

In 1983, she joined the team that became Ameritech Communications Inc. She formed the finance and human resources organizations as comptroller before being promoted to director of product management. In 1987, she became director of new business opportunity/systems integration. Her business unit was responsible for winning two of the largest competitive sales in the company's history, providing network management services to the State of Illinois and the City of Chicago. She was then appointed division manager of consumer affairs at Illinois Bell.

In 1989, Quandt joined Schneider Communications, a high-growth regional long-distance company as vice president of marketing. She was recruited by Call-Net Enterprises (Toronto) in 1992 as vice president of marketing and product development in the newly deregulated Canadian long-distance market. The operating company became Sprint Canada after forging an alliance with the U.S. carrier. Upon successful integration of the alliance, Quandt left to become CEO of Taylor Winfield Partners (Dallas), a consulting firm specializing in business strategy consulting and executive search for venture-backed high-technology start-ups.

In 1998, Quandt joined one of her start-up clients, 21st Century Telecom Group, a bundled communications provider, as senior vice president of marketing and sales. She was part of the management team that raised $300 million in debt financing for the first competitive cable TV company in Chicago. With the company's acquisition of EnterAct, Quandt was named president of the consumer sales group. She was responsible for the company's home and small business distribution channels for telephone, cable TV, and high-speed data. She retired in 1999 when RCN purchased the company.

In her "retirement," she joined two more start-ups in marketing and sales roles: BeMany!.com and maverix.net. She formed a real estate company and develops numerous properties in the Midwest. She is now managing partner of The ROI Partnership, a branding, product development, and sales strategy consulting firm.

Quandt is a candidate for a Ph.D. in organizational development at Benedictine University. She is an adjunct professor in the business school at the University of Wisconsin at Milwaukee. She holds an M.B.A. in finance from the University of Wisconsin at Whitewater and a B.S. in accounting from Valparaiso University. Her non-profit involvement has included board positions with Our Next Generation (chair), Imagine Chicago (chair), Leadership Greater Chicago, and Future Milwaukee, as well as co-founding Women Shaping Technology.

Index